DIARY OF MY ANALYSIS
WITH SIGMUND FREUD

DIARY OF MY ANALYSIS
WITH SIGMUND FREUD

by

Smiley Blanton, M.D.

With Biographical Notes and Comments
by Margaret Gray Blanton
Introduction by Iago Galdston, M.D.

HAWTHORN BOOKS, INC.   NEW YORK
W. Clement Stone, Publisher

DIARY OF MY ANALYSIS WITH SIGMUND FREUD

1 2 3 4 5 6 7 8 9 10

PREFACE

by Margaret Gray Blanton

When my husband, Dr. Smiley Blanton, died in October, 1966, at the age of eighty-four, he left among his manuscripts a diary of his analysis with Sigmund Freud. The diary consisted of about 120 typewritten pages. It covered the initial period of his analysis in Vienna from September, 1929, to June, 1930, and of three subsequent periods, of about two weeks each, in the summers of 1935, 1937, and 1938. The typewritten pages were transcripts made from the original entries jotted down in hard-covered notebooks from day to day as the analysis progressed.

Freud at that time accepted as patients only those who planned to become professional analysts. From the very start, therefore, the purpose of the diary was not to make a detailed record of a clinical case history. On the contrary, the entries consisted of selected highlights and noteworthy incidents of the analytical hour, and were intended to serve as the basis for a monograph on Freud's method of conducting an analysis. Freud knew about these notes and offered no objection whatever to any future use that my husband might make of them. In such matters, Freud held the view that every individual was completely free to write as he wished about his own personal experiences, including analysis.

Accordingly, it was my husband's plan to add background data, explanatory notes, and where necessary, further psychoanalytical comments that would make of the diary a rounded historical document of both general and scientific interest.

Apparently he never got around to the actual writing of this supplementary material. The heavy working schedule of a practicing analyst, of course, leaves little time for other professional undertakings of an extensive nature. But my husband did make use of his available free time to write half a dozen books, alone or in collaboration, as well as numerous papers and monographs, although he kept deferring work on the diary from year to year. It may be that there just was not enough time for everything he planned to write, or perhaps the delays were due to a natural hesitancy about including even the minimum of intimate personal history that one can hardly avoid setting down in a work of this kind.

Smiley's writing plan as he discussed it with me had been, first, a description of his first glimpse of the professor, more or less each time, as he felt that impression would be the freshest; next, what they said and did when they met; then any discussions of the didactics of analysis to follow. After that, dream material and the analytical work on it.

But in the manuscript as I found it, this latter part was very rudimentary. When the dream material was given, it was often very brief and merely followed by the words "and so forth." Discussion of this material was the part of his work that he was saving for a future day when he would tap his fantastic memory in a leisurely fashion. Of course, much of this did get into the manuscript but had to be cut by me in an arbitrary fashion, for I felt that such intimate material, unless fully explained, would only have been misleading.

In any case, the manuscript he left behind was only the central core of the finished work that was to be written around it. Yet, while admittedly incomplete, it remains in itself a possibly unique document in the psychoanalytic literature, for it provides what might be described as a series of snapshots showing Freud in action, as it were, in the role of an analyst with an analysand.

I know of no published work in which an attempt has been made to portray Freud in this particular aspect, and for that reason I believe this diary, however incomplete a version of what my husband intended it to be, has a scientific and historical value that merits publication in its present form.

It goes without saying that Smiley, wanting to become an analyst, would aspire to training by Freud. If there were a fountainhead, Freud was surely that, and such words as "the father of analysis" were suitably applied to him.

Smiley had read Freud's books with great eagerness as they came out, and he had been criticized much by the indifferently learned for believing that Freud knew what he was talking about.

There was another element in his eagerness to work with Freud himself. Smiley was a person with a minimum of prejudice, and he felt that here was an opportunity to get from a superior Jew sidelights on our own Judeo-Christian culture.

From an early age, Smiley had been an inveterate and rapid reader, so when his Sunday reading was limited by his Presbyterian family to the Bible and to Shakespeare, he was in no sense deprived. He set out to read the Bible from cover to cover, which he did twice. Shakespeare he not only read but memorized.

In the process of such Bible study, he very early formed his own religious convictions, and to the last they showed little deviation. He did not care for and never could be persuaded to accept any rigid man-made creed. His belief was founded on the basic conviction of the equality of men. And this penetrated all of his thinking to the last. He thought prejudice against Jews both "medieval" and "vulgar" and, on the part of a follower of Jesus, unthinkable.

A certain similarity and a certain difference between the professor (as he was almost universally referred to) and my husband were interesting and may shed a little light on their relationship.

The professor was brought up in the heyday of Vienna's dominance of the scientific and social world. Equipage drawn by marvelously selected and decorated horses, filled with emperors and various royalty, must have been commonplace sights to him. He must, many a time, have had to step from the pavements to permit the passage of these human peacocks. And being a member of a minority race, he must have been very conscious of such a necessity.

Smiley, on the other hand, was brought up in the Old South, only shortly after it had suffered a most devastating defeat in the Civil War, but with the advantage of being a member of the dominant race.

And yet in many ways this upbringing was similar. Smiley belonged to a most rigid Presbyterian family, whose ideas of the correct behavior ruled and limited a person in almost every direction.

In practical matters, the lives of these two men were astonishingly different. Smiley's "emperor's carriage" was a nicely polished buggy going up the rocky Tennessee pikes. His aristocracy was Lee and Jackson. The decorations that his heroes wore were the empty sleeves and peg legs of the old soldiers.

Their backgrounds were so very diversified that one

might be tempted to think of them as too far apart. But their associative resources were deep in the same material, and their meeting places were larger than their divisions, for they both still had Shakespeare and the Bible.

In the fall of 1927, Smiley left the University of Minnesota in Minneapolis, where he had organized the first child-guidance center in the United States to be connected with a city's public schools, to take up his new post at Vassar College in Poughkeepsie, New York. He had been invited to organize and direct Vassar's proposed nursery school, for which a new building had just been erected, and to give courses in child guidance at the college.

At Vassar, we built a house for ourselves in the belief that this would be our permanent location. By 1929, however, the situation that had developed at the college did not permit the fulfillment of Smiley's original plans, especially in regard to teaching. He therefore felt that a change in his professional career would have to be made, and he decided that he wanted to establish himself in New York City, where he would go into private practice as a psychoanalyst. He had worked in psychiatry at Johns Hopkins under Dr. Adolph Meyer and later received his diploma in neurology and psychological medicine from the Royal College of Physicians and Surgeons, of London. He now hoped to obtain the necessary additional training by going to Europe and studying with Freud, if this could be arranged.

Fortunately, with the kind assistance of Dr. George Amsden, who was second in charge at Bloomingdale Hospital while we were at Vassar, Smiley was able to put this plan into effect. Dr. Amsden and his wife had been our good friends ever since the days at Johns Hopkins, and when we found that Dr. Amsden was going to Budapest to study with Dr. Sandor Ferenczi, one of Freud's earliest and closest colleagues, we asked him to help in obtaining Freud's acceptance of Smiley for analysis.

Dr. Amsden busied himself on Smiley's behalf, the necessary letters of recommendation were obtained, and finally Freud wrote to say that he could arrange for Smiley to start his analysis at the beginning of September. Another American, Dr. McCord, was finishing his analysis at that time, thus leaving the hour open on Freud's schedule.

A year's leave of absence had been arranged with Vassar, and late in the summer of 1929 we took a ten-day ship to London. From there I went over to Paris, while Smiley traveled directly to Berchtesgaden, where Freud had been spending the summer, and began the course of training for his new work. Later on we remet in Vienna.

It is my hope that this book will also be of special interest as one observer's personal sidelight on the great founder of psychoanalysis in the last years of his life.

I have supplied introductory and explanatory notes to acquaint the reader, where it seemed necessary, with background events and circumstances at the time of the analysis. These are in no sense intended to take the place of the personal psychoanalytical notes and comments that my husband planned to write. They are given simply as a frame of reference to help put the diary in historical perspective.

—Margaret Gray Blanton
Nashville, Tennessee

CONTENTS

INTRODUCTION
by Iago Galdston, M.D.

What was it like to be Freud's patient, the analysand of the creator of psychoanalysis? The query is the more intriguing when directed to the patient who was himself a psychiatrist.

Freud had a long professional career. He treated patients literally up to the time of his terminal disablement and death. His patients were numerous, yet there are but few patients' reports on their treatment with Freud.

This is in measure quite understandable. The patient, deeply involved in his own therapy, is hardly in a position to stand off and critically observe the treatment process. Nor can he objectively study the analyst with whom he is engaged in an emotional interaction.

Freud discouraged (did not forbid) public as well as private revelations of what went on during the analytic hour. It is not that Freud wanted to keep *it* secret, but rather because no third party—unless he could be privy to *everything* that went into the interactions between the analysand and analyst, which of course is utterly impossible—could possibly appreciate and understand what in effect did take place, factually and dynamically. Freud adequately expounded in books and articles the processes of psychoanalysis, citing specific cases, but this was the therapist's story, not the patient's. In recent years some few venturesome ex-patients, in the main professional publicists, have written about their analyses. Some of their recitations are interest-

ing to read, but in effect they are seldom more than carica-
tures or somewhat fictional sketches of their therapeutic
experiences.

But what of the psychiatric analysand? Only a few have
written of their experience with Freud, and as was to be
expected, they tell more of Freud the person than of Freud
the therapist, less of their case histories and more of the
impression Freud made on them. Reading such "revelations"—those, say, of Adolf Stern, Roy Grinker, and to add
an odd one, that of Joseph Wortis—one is impressed with
the fact that, as was to be expected, what was observed
depended upon the personality and character of the observer. Such "revelations" do not, however, add up to a
paradox portrait but rather to a portrait in depth of Freud's
complex personality.

It is to this portrait that Smiley Blanton's *Diary of My
Analysis with Sigmund Freud* makes a unique and precious
contribution. For Blanton himself was unique and precious.
My more than thirty years of intimate association with
Smiley convinced me of this.

I first encountered Smiley in the late twenties. I was at
that time teaching a course at New York University on the
behavior problems of children. I was badly in need of a
relevant textbook, and in my search I came upon the work
recently published by Smiley and Margaret Blanton titled
Child Guidance. I was much impressed with this book and
adopted it as a text.

Smiley was at that time working and teaching at Vassar.
Shortly thereafter I learned that Smiley had left Vassar and
was living in New York City. I invited him to address my
student group, and he willingly did so. At this, our first
meeting, I was much drawn to the man. He was not only
well informed, thoughtful, and original, but also transpar-

ently sincere and sympathetic. He had a playful humor which he could exercise without hostility, yet he was forthright in his condemnations of malice, pretense, and fraud. There was a great deal of the exuberant boy in him, even in his older years, and much also of the poet.

I recall one interesting incident that mirrors Smiley's qualities as a person. When Smiley was still a newcomer, I once asked A. A. Brill what he thought of Smiley. Brill responded that at first he'd had his reservations. Smiley was treating a young schizophrenic whom Brill considered unsuited for individual therapy. Was he doing this for financial reasons? Then, Brill discovered that Smiley was treating the boy without charge. His motive was to see what he could do with the seemingly hopeless youngster.

Another incident is of interest. At about the time of the above-cited experience, I was asked to treat a young woman who was an interesting and accomplished person, member of a distinguished family. I thought it best not to undertake to treat her because I was too intimately involved with some of the senior members of her family. I referred her instead to Smiley, who did take her in therapy with excellent results. The point in this recitation is that Smiley at this time had no patients, and the one I referred to him was either the first or among the first he had in the city. Of course I had no idea of this when I referred the case to him, but Smiley construed my action as one of great consideration, and periodically and embarrassingly swamped me with unmerited gratitude. He was indeed a most generous soul!

Smiley's relations with the Reverend Norman Vincent Peale, his studies together with Margaret Blanton of the "miraculous cures" at Lourdes, his lifelong interest in poetry and dramatic literature, his fondness for animals in general and for birds in particular—all these are facets of this unique individual whose notes on his analysis with Freud are here published. These notes bring no new or startling revelations, but they do proffer the pleasure of seeing one rare and great man through the eyes of another.

—Iago Galdston, M.D.

DIARY OF MY ANALYSIS
WITH SIGMUND FREUD

BERCHTESGADEN
GRAND HOTEL

September 1, 1929

I saw Professor Freud yesterday for the first time, my appointment being for three o'clock. I was much chagrined to be late. My taxi driver, despite his reassurances when we started from the hotel, proved not to know the location of Freud's house, and it was twenty minutes past three before we finally found it.

I had developed quite a bit of anxiety about starting my analysis. As part of the resistance, I had cut my finger slightly in the morning and had also suffered a moderately severe attack of indigestion, to which I am subject when under nervous or emotional strain.

Freud lives in a small villa in the pine woods about four miles from Berchtesgaden. I went up on the porch but was unable to find a bell or knocker. The front door was open, however, and I rapped timidly on the glass pane. After a wait of two or three minutes, I heard someone moving in the room just off the hall. A few seconds later, a frail, small-statured, gray-haired man with a gray beard appeared in the hallway and came toward me. Although he looked older than in the photographs I had seen, I recognized the approaching figure to be that of Freud himself. He was carrying a cigar in his hand, and there was something almost diffident in his manner as he addressed me.

"Is this Doctor Blanton?" he said in a low voice. His

articulation was somewhat indistinct, doubtless due to the operations he has undergone for cancer of the upper right jawbone. When I replied in the affirmative, he added, "I thought the appointment was at three o'clock."

There was no irritation in his voice, but I felt that he was sizing me up, wondering what sort of person I was and why I should keep him waiting. In the meantime he had asked me into his room just off the hall. I explained a bit breathlessly how the taxi driver had failed to find the place. At the same time, I handed the professor the letter which Dr. McCord had asked me to give Freud as soon as I saw him.

"As I see your name mentioned," said Freud, after motioning me to a seat, "I will read the letter."

I looked about the room. It was very plain, the floor bare save for a small rug. A desk was in front of the window. To the right of the desk and against the wall was a comfortable couch with blankets on it and a shawl or soft woolen blanket folded on the head end. Behind the couch was a leather-covered chair with a straight back.

After reading the letter, Freud motioned me to the couch, while he took the chair at the head.

"You have written and spoken about analysis," he began inquiringly. I hastened to say that I had not.

"But you have read about it."

"Oh, yes," I replied.

"Well, how is it carried on?"

I replied that the patient lies on the couch, with the analyst seated at his head, and freely speaks all that comes into his mind. I mentioned also that the patient should be completely relaxed. In point of fact, however, I was half sitting, half lying on the couch, rather tensely.

"Well, then," said Freud, "why don't you relax?" I

stretched out in a more comfortable position.

While Freud was reading the letter, he smoked in small puffs, frequently taking the cigar from his mouth to champ his teeth as though his dental plate hurt him.

After I had relaxed, Freud said, "You may wonder why I make so few comments, or help you so little."

I then began to give Freud the thoughts that were in my mind. First I discussed the chagrin I felt in being late. Then I told him that I was happy to be with him, that I had always liked him and disliked Jung and Adler. When Freud asked me why, I said I did not quite know but simply felt that way.

I then spoke of my feeling of insecurity. "About what?" asked Freud.

"About my life in general," I answered, and then suggested that I had best give him a history of my past life. Freud agreed, and so I drew a brief outline of my life. Occasionally Freud interrupted to question me about some of the points that came up. At all times he seemed in close touch with what I was saying. I felt he was interested, that he was taking in what I was giving him. There was none of that cold detachment which I had imagined was the attitude an analyst is supposed to take.

As we went along, Freud's simple manner made me feel secure and easy. At the same time, there was a detachment which was not repelling but pleasant. I talked until I heard a clock strike four. I rose at once, stopping in the middle of my sentence.

"I am sorry the hour was so short," said Freud as he accompanied me into the hall. He asked if I knew my way to the station, and I assured him that I did. Then I said, "May I ask how long you shall remain here?"

"I leave on the 15th of September," Freud replied, "but

I go to Berlin for a month." With a shrug, he added, "You can either accompany me, or you can wait until I return to Vienna."

I assured him that I should accompany him, since I wished to do as much work with him as possible while I was in Europe. I shook his hand and departed after confirming that our next session will be on Monday. Freud does not work on Sunday.

The impressions that stand out after this first meeting are Freud's smallness of stature (about 5'4", I should judge), his soft and almost deprecating manner, the way in which he makes you feel at ease yet combines this with a detachment which leaves you free to express yourself. I also got the impression of frailness. He is partly bald, his head is not large, and his forehead, while high, is not as high as mine. I should add that his command of English is superb, luckily for an American who knows almost no German.

September 2, 1929

I was on time today. I went out on the 2:15 electric, walked to the house, and waited on the grass for 29 minutes before going up on the porch, where I sat in a chair for a few minutes until Freud came out and asked me in. His manner was cordial and friendly but detached.

I immediately lay down on the couch, and Freud seated himself as before at the head.

"Go ahead as though this were a new time," Freud began, "and not the continuation of last time."

I started by saying that I felt my mucous colitis and finger-cutting (I cut my finger again this morning) were caused by resistance.

"Perhaps," said Freud. "There are many motives. Resistance is perhaps one of them." He meant, of course, that resistance was one of the motives that caused the colitis and the cutting.

I then began to explain why I liked him and disliked Jung and Adler. I said that he was an artist as well as a scientist, that I disliked Jung because of the moral factor that he drags in, and Adler because he got credit for doing what I had done in the Minneapolis schools.

"What have you read of my works?" asked Freud.

"All published in English."

"They have not all been translated into English," he commented. Then he asked what I had read of Jung and Adler. I told him.

Next I began to give a brief account of my life and training.

Freud interrupted me: "Have you prepared this?"

"Yes," I replied.

"But," said Freud, "you must not prepare what you are to say but give freely what comes into your mind. That is the classical method."

I was silent for several moments—whereupon Freud said, "You may go ahead and give me what you have prepared!" He asked a few questions about dates and did not understand the word "Argonne" until I repeated it several times.

Apropos of something, Freud asked me if I had any children. When I said no, he made a sympathetic remark or rather exclamation. I spoke of my dog Bobs and of my affection for him.

"The feeling for dogs is the same as we have for children; it is of the same quality," said Freud. "But do you know in what way it differs? . . . There is no ambivalence, no element of hostility."

I remarked that there seemed at times to be some element of hostility, as when the dog wanted to go out and I was tired and did not want to.

"This feeling of hostility is not such as we have toward our children," said Freud.

I acquiesced. But I still think Freud is not correct in saying that we have no ambivalence toward dogs. They do demand things and disobey and disappoint us, and so give rise to a certain amount of hostility.

I mentioned at one point that I could not remember names. "Ah," said Freud. I tried to remember the name of one of his books that I used in my classes, saying that the scene was laid in Rome. "Perhaps," suggested Freud, "it was in Pompeii." He was right, and the book turned out to be *Gradiva.* I then spoke of Dr. Salmon. In reply to some statement of mine, Freud said that "it is almost universally thought that he committed suicide."

I paused and then remarked that I thought of my childhood and the autumn days like these. Freud rose as he said, "Then perhaps you will like it here."

I did not realize that the hour was up; I expected the clock to chime. Actually, it was five minutes before four. Freud accompanied me to the door, saying, "Tomorrow at the same time, then." I replied that this would be very convenient, and Freud hurried out onto the porch as though he were going to meet another patient.

I felt a little depressed and disappointed. I don't know why; nothing had been said or done to depress me. Perhaps it was the knowledge that I must soon plunge into the midst of my real difficulties and frailties. Another impression I carried away was the difficulty Freud had in speaking. Several times I could not understand what he said, even though he repeated it more than once. Perhaps this is due somewhat to resistances on my part; perhaps I shall get used to his speech as time goes on.

I must mention that during the hour I remarked that I could not be analyzed by someone who did not have wisdom and an appreciation of the nuances of life. Then I told Freud the joke about the man who had shook the hand that shook the hand of John L. Sullivan. Freud was much amused.

I also spoke of how sorry I felt for poor mud turtles (I called them tortoises) when they had to carry their heavy shells as they walked.

"Perhaps the turtle does not feel as badly as you think," said Freud.

I spoke of my finickiness about food and sensitiveness to noise, adding that by will power I had conquered this while I was in the army. I said, "This shows what can be done by will power when you try."

"Sometimes," said Freud, to which I added, "Yes, when you engage the unconscious on your side." To this Freud agreed.

In the course of the hour, Freud asked me whether I did any artistic writing, meaning stories or other fiction. (He had asked this when I told of how, at Harvard, I tried to write a story about a Negro boy whom the other boys made fun of.) I replied that I had tried but found I was not good enough. Perhaps, I added, that was why I went into psychiatry.

September 3, 1929

I was almost late today. I walked out and had to run to get there on time. I barely made it by one minute.

Freud met me in the hall and with his usual somewhat deprecating bow pointed to the chair for me to place my hat and stick. We went in, he motioning me as usual to go first. I immediately lay down, apologizing for my dusty shoes. Waving aside my apology, Freud asked if I had prepared anything. I replied that I had not; I found I had a tendency to do so but resolutely put the idea out of my mind.

I talked of my prejudice toward Germans and the great amount of hate there was in the world. I also regretted the fact that I had been misled into believing all lies told about the Germans. Freud commented that there were many more who did the same thing. I spoke so fast at this point that Freud stopped me and asked that I speak in a lower voice and more slowly. He said it was difficult for him to understand when I spoke so rapidly.

I then spoke of Margaret and of our unhappiness over not having children. Freud seemed much interested in my description of Margaret and asked several questions. I mentioned her theory that the female orgasm was not the definite affair usually pictured. Freud remarked that what she thought was what was usually written. I said this was not the case with the books we read, which were not the usual ones.

I spoke of Margaret's analysis having been started by Clara Thompson. Freud immediately asked me to repeat the name, saying he did not know of her. I said Clara had been analyzed by Ferenczi. "Ah," said Freud in a tone of satisfaction.

At that point the hour was up. Freud rose and said, "It was much better. You were much freer than before," and bowed me out.

September 4, 1929

Very interesting hour with Freud today. I was still suffering from colitis. I had eaten no luncheon and was very tired. Freud was especially gracious. I think he likes me and finds me interesting. In fact, he said so—"It is very interesting"—when I was through today. I had talked of money and of my financial affairs, mentioning that I had $20,000. "When I was your age," said Freud, "I did not have so much."

I asked Freud if Margaret, who had saved up $1,000, could find an analyst at a fee of five to ten dollars an hour. He said that would be sufficient.

I talked of the Vassar situation, adding that I was not going to stay there but planned to go into practice in New York City. I explained that I did not want to submit to the narrow program of that particular women's college. Freud made an exclamation; it was not exactly a word, but it expressed his agreement with my decision.

When I remarked that I did not feel any doubt about my getting on, Freud said, "I have been astonished at your frequent changes. I should have thought that with your feeling of insecurity you would have remained in one place."

I spoke of doctors making money without giving adequate return and wondered about the situation between H.

and Dr. Q. Freud tried to help me pronounce Q's name correctly. Then he said, "Do you know how he does it?" I waited. "He commits his indiscretions when he is in his manic phase, and in his depressive phases he treats his patients. But," he went on, "he suffers for it in his depressions."

The clock struck four, and I rose, although again it was actually five minutes before the hour. "As you will," said Freud, spreading out his hands, and then adding, "That is very interesting. You must be patient. We will get to the deeper layers, and then I shall not be so silent, I shall give more of myself."

I forgot to note that I spoke of my bald head, commenting that I was bald at 21 but did not mind because I had a well-shaped head. "Yes," said Freud, "I have noticed that."

When I began to speak of my money affairs, Freud remarked that this was "the anal side." I confessed that I was somewhat embarrassed in speaking of this because I was afraid it would influence him in his charges.

"You must not let your critical side interfere with what comes into your mind," he cautioned.

I said something about how lucky I was to be with him, to which he replied, "Dr. Amsden wrote so well of you that I was glad to have you." Here I remarked that I had made many sacrifices to come over. "I know you have," said Freud, "and I hope you will be repaid for your sacrifice."

I then spoke of my desire for a school where superior boys would be trained, with a faculty of teachers who had all been analyzed. Freud said, "That would be very important." He added something else, to the effect that the idea was a good one and such a school would be helpful.

When I spoke again of my colitis, Freud said perhaps it was caused by the heat. *Not once has he suggested that it was due to resistance.* *

September 5, 1929

I showed much resistance today by talking about superficial things. Freud seemed somewhat bored. Perhaps this is not the right word. Anyhow, he was not satisfied.

I was criticizing myself about being a baby. Freud said, "You know one of the chief ways that resistance shows itself? . . . In blaming and criticizing yourself."

Toward the end of the hour, Freud said, "May I ask you an indiscreet question: How do you sleep at night?" I replied that I slept poorly, waking up every two hours throughout the night.

"Do you dream?"

"Yes, frequently. I had a dream last night."

"Why did you not tell it?"

"Because I wanted to wait until I could write it down as soon as I awakened," I replied.

"But you must not do this," said Freud. "To write the

*Smiley and I were in analysis at the same time. Sometimes the road was very long and very rough. Both of us had what might be called heightened sensibilities or, in common speech, a chip on the shoulder.

One day he said something that angered me, and I countered with the worst insult I could think of: "You must be in a state of negative transference." And I added, "I bet you won't repeat this conversation to the professor!"

He cooled off for a moment and then said, "You only show how little you know. You don't have to tell him what your state of resistance is. As a matter of fact, he says that both the negative and the positive transferences are part of the analytical process and in no way to be feared. That they are there to be worked through."—M.G.B.

dream down increases the resistance, so that it is often impossible to analyze it. No. Do not write the dream down. If the resistance takes it away, let it do so."

I started to recall a dream I had some time ago, but he stopped me.

"We must have recent dreams, ones that you have had the night before," he said. "But we will keep this one you had last night and use it tomorrow if you do not have another one."

I wanted to give him the outline of the dream, but he said it was too late to begin, as the hour was up.

As I was leaving, he put his hand on my arm and said, "For an analyst not to tell his dreams is a nice bit of resistance!"

During the hour I spoke of my pain at seeing the suffering and poverty in London. "What will you think of the poverty in Vienna!" Freud interjected. I said that my feeling was very much like what I had when I felt sorry for the boy with the receding chin whom I saw at school when I was six. Then I remarked that perhaps my feeling was due to an overcompensation for a sadism. "But," I added, "I suppose there must be some fundamental feelings or sympathies not caused by compensations."

"Yes, of course," said Freud.

Freud has a way of making a certain kind of sound in his throat—a sort of grunt or exclamation—to indicate that he agrees or sympathizes with you, without talking so much that you are hindered in your flow.

I almost forgot to note that Freud said, "If you are studying your own dreams, you must write them down. But that is not the thing for your patients to do. I used to have my patients write their dreams down, but I am sure it is the wisest plan not to do so."

30

September 6, 1929

Had a very interesting session today. In the midst of analyzing my dream, Freud asked, "Do you know why you have so much resistance?"

"No—unless the dream has some connection with my sexual life," I replied.

"No, it is probably connected with your analysis," said Freud. "I have found that the car in dreams often means the analysis. I am not sure, but it seems that this might be so. And the man who is driving may be me."

I said perhaps this might be so, but I could hardly believe that I regarded Freud in such an unfavorable light, even in my unconscious mind.

"Why not?" Freud countered.

I suggested that the association might mean I was afraid I would be cheated in my analysis by not getting what I came for. Freud replied that probably this was so.

As I left, Freud remarked, "You see how much more interesting it is when you associate with your dreams."

Again I am impressed by Freud's soft and easy manner. He does not push you. He does not make emphatic statements often. When he does, it is in a very undominating manner. I feel easy with him.

September 7, 1929

This is my 8th day with Freud.

While analyzing my dreams, I began to give reasons for

my actions as brought out by the associations.

Freud stopped me. "Do not give the reasons," he said. "They will come out in time. When a person tells me something, I do not try to think of the reasons. I know that the reasons will appear in time. There is a saying which I think comes from Oliver Cromwell: 'You never get so high as when you don't know where you are going.' It is so in analysis."

I spoke about something I had done, and said it would look bad to state it without the surrounding circumstances.

Freud replied, "It is the fact that is important, is it not?"

September 9, 1929

On Saturday I had much resistance and did not get very far.

"The way to treat resistance," said Freud, "is to let it grow until it defeats itself. Today has been absolutely sterile." But in order to encourage me, he said as I departed, "It takes time to develop the right attitude and to overcome resistance. But I am sure you will be of much assistance in helping us to overcome it."

At one point during the hour, Freud asked me if Jews were not put in the same category as Negroes. I said I had not met with this comparison. Freud said, "I often have."

September 10, 1929

I showed Freud a notice in the N. Y. *Herald* about Adler going to Columbia University to lecture this winter. Freud commented that the picture did not look like Adler. I spoke of my dislike of Adler. "Well," said Freud, "you must find out if your dislike of Adler is based on some sound scientific grounds or on some more personal grounds."

I said that Emerson had written about compensation many years ago and that Adler had not added anything to our knowledge of behavior.

"If a man takes an old idea," said Freud, "and develops it and makes it grander, that is worthwhile." Later he remarked, "Do you know why Adler is succeeding in America? . . . It is because he is capitalizing on the opposition to analysis. In the case of Jung, that is another matter."

I observed that Jung's latest book was full of mysticism. "Yes, Jung believes all that about spirits," said Freud.

I told Freud that I thought analysis would spread widely in America in the next ten years. "No," he replied, "I think it will take twenty to thirty years—a generation, I give it." I demurred from this.

Freud said something about how eager America was to take up fads like Couéism or like Adler's work. I said that W. F., with his watered-down analysis, was hurting the movement.

"We shall always have such men," said Freud.

I said I believed that the movement would grow faster than he, Freud, said it would, that I had faith.

Freud replied, "You should have, you are so much younger."

I had three dreams. Freud asked me to give them all, and commented, "You have cut down your dreams from seven to three."

I associated, at his request, with the first dream. It was about my fear of analysis. At the end of the hour, Freud said, "You see, one dream is enough for the hour."

I am impressed with how little help Freud gives. He often says nothing for 10 to 15 minutes. It is a matter of growth, and I must go ahead and work it out as best I can.

September 16, 1929

Did not have a chance to write up my account of Friday's meeting with Freud.

Had a most interesting session today. Freud talked most of the hour, or at least half of it. After I had given the associations to some numbers in Friday's dream, Freud said:

"There is this rule in analysis: *The analyst should never bother himself to find out the exact meaning of the patient.* He need not concern himself about this. Let him only help the patient to overcome his resistances, and the patient will eventually find out the meaning. If the analyst tries to force the patient to find out the meaning, or if the analyst tries to help the patient, he increases the resistance of the patient."

I was reluctant to mention some of the unconscious associations and began to give excuses.

Freud interrupted me, saying, "May I give you what seems to be a rule of analysis?" He then repeated the admonition about giving free reign to the unconscious, without reservations. "You are not responsible for your unconscious," he said. "But while you are bringing up the material, you must not have any moral judgments about it.

"The unconscious," he continued, "must have its day in court along with the conscious mind. It is only when both have expressed themselves that you are able to make your judgments as to what you wish to do. And it is only when you have laid self-criticism aside, and when you do not care what the analyst thinks, that you are able to get at the depth of the unconscious. Self-criticism is a form of inhibition. And excuses for the unconscious may lead to insecurity. For it is only a step from excusing the material from the unconscious to being insecure in telling what is in the unconscious."*

---

*From the middle of September to nearly the end of October, Freud stayed at Dr. Ernst Simmel's psychoanalytical sanatorium in Tegel, on the outskirts of Berlin, while his surgeon repaired the prosthesis which had been giving Freud so much trouble. Although Smiley followed the professor to Berlin, as planned, no diary notes for this period were found, and the next entry appears after they returned to Vienna.

The only written reference to this interval was a brief notation that I made of my first meeting with Freud, which took place at that time. I went to Berlin with Smiley and accompanied him to Tegel one hot September afternoon for my appointment with the professor. I was never Freud's patient, since—as I have previously noted—he accepted only those who planned to become analysts. I went to the conference simply as Smiley's wife, and our meeting lasted about five minutes.

With simple directness, this slight, frail-looking little man made me feel that the five minutes was to be a conference between two equally important (or unimportant) human beings. I made no record of our conversation, but I remember how Freud looked past the untidy appearance produced by my dusty walk to the sanatorium, saw the face underneath, and also, I daresay, saw through the face. Had I entered with any idea of dissimulation, I would have given it up, for he seemed to me, more than anyone I had ever met, to come at the truth quickly. After I had gone out of the room, indeed, I became aware of a feeling that I had been in the presence of a man of great magnitude. That reaction does not always follow a first contact with greatness.—M.G.B.

November 9, 1929

For a long time I have been giving only dreams at the sessions with Freud. Two days ago, he said, "Are you not fed up with dreams? You need to give also what is in your conscious mind."

Today I gave two short dreams which were full of meaning. "You see," said Freud, "it is not necessary that a dream be a mile long in order for it to be valuable."

I said it was hard to go through analysis.

"I think people who practice analysis, or who have read the literature, often make their own analysis difficult," replied Freud. "They lack naïveté. The analyst should realize that the unconscious mind does not have the opposites that the conscious mind has. In the conscious we have black and white, but in the unconscious we do not have such opposites. It is necessary for the unconscious to express itself freely. When we find unmoral attitudes or qualities, do not try to bring out their opposites. Let us appreciate that we are unmoral, savage beings in the unconscious.

"This does not detract at all from our human moral dignity and moral achievement," he continued. "Eventually, when the unconscious has expressed itself freely, we can reconcile the two sides. But it must not be done prematurely, nor on every occasion when the unconscious expresses itself must we bring up the opposite. If we do, we intimidate the unconscious. It must be free to express itself."

Later in the hour, Freud repeated, *"There is nothing in analysis to detract from human achievement and moral dignity."**

*This is the last entry for 1929. Any additional entries were either lost or discarded, or perhaps the analytical sessions during the next two months were held, for whatever reason, on an irregular schedule. In notes he made for a lecture given at Union College in later years, however, Smiley refers to a session in

DIARY OF MY ANALYSIS WITH SIGMUND FREUD

January 22, 1930

This evening I said to Freud, in discussing my temperament, that I was of an enthusiastic type. I mentioned that I was reading the *Interpretation of Dreams* and how thrilled I was by the drama of the thing: A poor Jewish doctor—who was looked upon by his colleagues as a crackpot, who had

---

December, 1929, when the subject of Shakespeare's plays came up. Smiley's account of the discussion is as follows:

"Do you think Shakespeare wrote Shakespeare?" Freud said to me.
"Do you mean the man born at Stratford-on-Avon—did he write the plays attributed to him?"
"Yes," he replied.
I told Freud that I had specialized in English and drama for twelve years before I went into medicine, had been on the stage for a year or so, and had memorized a half dozen of Shakespeare's dramas, and I could see no reason to doubt that the Stratford man had written the plays.
"Well," said Freud, "here's a book I would like you to read. This man believes someone else wrote the plays."
I was very much upset. I thought to myself that if Freud believes Bacon or Ben Jonson or anyone else wrote Shakespeare's plays, I would not have any confidence in his judgment and could not go on with my analysis. So I asked my wife to read the book and tell me what she thought.

The book turned out to be J. Thomas Looney's *'Shakespeare' Identified in Edward De Vere, 17th Earl of Oxford.* On this particular day, Smiley was carrying it under his arm when he joined me at the café where it was our custom to meet after his analytical hour. He seemed very disturbed and depressed and spoke of his qualms about continuing with Freud. Handing me the book, he said, "Will you help me out and read this?"
Fortunately, by that time I had had enough analysis to recognize the resistance phenomenon when I saw it. I was glad to read the book, however, for it proved to be a thoroughly sound work, based on solid scholarship, and its subject was approached with exemplary scientific objectivity. Whether or not one agreed with its thesis—that the Earl of Oxford was the actual author of the plays—it was obviously a book to command respectful attention.
Smiley was relieved to hear my verdict and then read the book himself. Although he remained unconvinced by its argument, he recognized at once that the book was a serious work and not just another Baconian exercise in secret ciphers and codes. The crisis was passed, and he went on with his analysis.
Thereafter we sent the professor new books on this subject whenever they were published in the United States. Freud always wrote to thank us for the books, and in time it was to make a sort of small link between us which we valued.—*M.G.B.*

given up his chances of advancement for his beliefs, with only the support of his faithful patients—solves the problem of the meaning of dreams, and then, one summer's day, sits down and begins his epoch-making book with "I shall prove . . ."—not "shall attempt" or "endeavor," but "I shall *prove*."

This, I said, was high drama, ranking with the great moments in human thought, with Descartes' famous *Cogito* and St. Paul's appeal before King Agrippa. (And I should have added, as my wife suggested, with Luther's famous nailing of his articles on the door of the church.)

"Well, I did not feel, at the time, that it was so dramatic," Freud replied. "I had no idea of being dogmatic or of challenging the world; it seemed that was the simplest way to put it."

I ventured to suggest that this is doubtless the way all great men feel. "And after thirty years," I continued, "it seems the best minds of the world have been unable to modify the book in any essential. I presume that you still hold to what has been written in your book."

Freud replied, "I am getting out an eighth edition, and the main structure of the book remains unchanged."

January 23, 1930

I spoke of the problem I had this summer to teach mental hygiene and yet not be superficial.

In substance, Freud said, "It seems to me that it would be well to avoid superficial formulations when you are teaching the relation of psychoanalysis to education and mental hygiene. It is best to teach fundamental facts. You have an opportunity to show how superficial is Adler's doctrine of inferiority complex. A child feels inferior not because he has an inferior organ or organs, but because he is not loved. *It is the parent's attitude toward the child's inferior organ that causes the difficulty.*"

Here Freud gave me an example:

"You know Emil Ludwig, who wrote the life of Kaiser Wilhelm. Well, he was here for dinner with me, and I asked him why he was so superficial, why he analyzed the whole personality of the Kaiser on the basis of an inferiority due to his withered arm. I told him it was not this which caused the inferiority but Wilhelm's mother's attitude toward the withered arm. It is an historical fact that Wilhelm's mother hated him. She despised him because of his withered arm. . . . Ludwig did not like my criticism."

Freud went on to say, "The child who is really loved does not feel inferior. And this attitude depends mostly on the mother. She deals with the child mostly during the first years of life. The father's influence is generally of no very great importance.

"The child's desire for attention," he continued, "is only a diminished desire for love. It is not attention that the child is seeking but love. Of course, a child must sometimes be thwarted. But if this thwarting occurs in a background of love, it will cause no harmful effects. The fundamental principle of psychoanalysis in education is the question of the *economics of love.** Training is a question of

*In September, 1938, I asked Freud if he had ever used this phrase in any of his publications. He said, "No."

how to give the child the right amount of love."

(Anna Freud* said in one of her hours, "Right training is a question of the right mixture of satisfaction and deprivation. If a child is completely satisfied, he will remain fixed at this level.")

Freud continued, "Another difficulty is that parents expect their children to carry out their own unfulfilled desires —infantile desires and wishes."

"Children feel when people love them," I said, "through muscle tensions."

"Perhaps," replied Freud, "but it is well to avoid physiological conceptions when we are dealing with psychological levels."

"Teachers so often hate their children!" I remarked.

"Yes, an education of hate must be replaced by an education of love. Of course," continued Freud, "there are other elements in the case of the child who seeks too much attention or who fantasizes too much. In the case of the girl, she feels some hate toward the mother when she realizes that she has not been given a penis. When she has a brother, she feels that he is loved more by the mother because he was given a penis; she then feels unloved. In the case of the boy, the threats of castration make him feel unloved. All of these elements come into the case and must be considered if the formulation is not to be too superficial."

On another occasion, while discussing female psychology, Freud said, "You will find in analysis that nearly every girl identifies herself with her mother, real or imaginary. This may not occur at first, but it occurs sooner or later. Even when the daughters hate their mothers, this identification occurs. It is for this reason that it is hard to prophesy

*Sigmund Freud's daughter.—*Ed.*

what a girl's character will be in later life. It generally occurs that there is a marked change after she has experienced sex relations. So that in cases where the girl is a virgin, there is generally a marked change in her character after marriage." He paused a moment and then concluded, "Picking a wife is one of the most difficult things in this civilization."

February 13, 1930

During a recent session with Freud, I mentioned that I was saving up to buy a copy of his works. "I've been a teacher all my life," I said, "and I don't have much money."

Next day Freud said to me, "May I present you with a copy of my books?" Whereupon he gave me a set of his *Collected Papers,* in four volumes. As he did so, he remarked that these papers were the foundation of psychoanalysis and implied that I would benefit by reading them.

This seems to have set in motion a series of rather elaborate dreams on subsequent nights. I dreamed of the war, of soldiers fighting to defend a railway station, of a frisky dog hitched to a box full of cartridges and hauling it between rows of pillars holding up the station roof.

I had all kinds of associations: of the station in Nancy which the Germans used to bomb every night; of the packing boxes I had had built to move our books some years ago —and so equated the ammunition with Freud's books; the defense of the railroad station with defense of psychoanalysis against its attackers; of the station pillars with the pillars of society who would not accept Freud's books if they really knew how revolutionary these were and what an explosion they could cause.

There were other dreams: of the campus at Vassar; of my dog Bobs; of someone asking me to recite, which I do, quoting the passage from Shakespeare about the poet's pen, which "gives to airy nothing" a "local habitation and a name." Here, again, my associations led to Freud's books and my equating him with Shakespeare.

February 14, 1930

Yesterday I could get nothing from my dreams.

"For the past few days," said Freud, "your dreams have been growing more and more obscure. This can have only one meaning: There is a change in the transference. It is probably due to the present of the books. You will see from this what difficulties gifts in analysis always make."

February 20, 1930

Yesterday Freud asked if I had ever heard of Dr. A. A. Roback, onetime instructor in psychology who had written a book about the place of Jews in literature, art, and science. Handing me a copy, Freud said, "The book is not worth much, so just glance it over."

I read the book and thought it was pompous as well as not very good. In the section on psychoanalysis, Roback made it appear that psychoanalysis was a product of the Jewish mind. I asked Freud about this.

"My background as a Jew helped me to stand being criticized, being isolated, working alone," Freud replied. "All this was of help to me in discovering analysis. But that psychoanalysis itself is a Jewish product seems to me nonsense. As a scientific work, it is neither Jewish nor Catholic nor Gentile."

I said I felt the same way and added that the Scotch were quite like the Jews in their mysticism, their desire to find a purpose for life.

At this, Freud remarked, "I had not read Roback's discussion of myself. I noticed in glancing over this part that he said I was a mystic. This seems to me to be amusing—I think I am farthest from being a mystic."

I mentioned that Roback had quoted from Wittels' book about his (Freud's) attempt to put Jung at the head of psychoanalysis.

"Yes, that was true," Freud replied. "At the time, I felt that people would think of psychoanalysis as a Jewish movement. Now, Roback is not unfriendly to psychoanalysis, yet he thinks of it as a Jewish movement—so you see I was right. . . . But Jung proved to be a failure."

I said, "I think your own personality was a better starting point for psychoanalysis than that of any other person."

"There was a danger that people would consider psychoanalysis as primarily Jewish," said Freud.

"This would have occured in any case," I replied. "If Janet had discovered psychoanalysis, the world would have said, 'Yes, it is due to the wicked French, who have no morals.' Or if German, they would have said, 'Due to the crude German mind.' "

"Yes," agreed Freud. "In the case of syphilis, it was

called the Naples disease in France. The Turks called it the Frankish disease, and so on."

I remarked that Jung had said psychoanalysis was a Jewish product and that Christians needed another psychology.

"Yes," said Freud. "This was after Jung had accepted psychoanalysis. His change was a deliberate attempt to change for the benefit of the American public."

February 24, 1930

I went to dancing class yesterday, from five to six. I stopped at 5:45, but talked to Kitty, my dancing partner, until 5:50 about my next appointments. Not being able to get a taxi at the door, I was four minutes late for analysis.

I was quite flustered about it. When I went into the waiting room, the outside door to the consulting room was open, but the inside door was closed. The maid asked me to go in.

Freud was in his library, smoking. He was quite composed and kindly, as though I had not been late, but I was still flustered. As I lay down, I pulled out my watch and said, "I am afraid my watch is a little slow. I had best set it by yours."

"My watch is usually right," he replied, but he did not give me the time. Instead he asked, "You were at dancing school?"

"Yes," I said. "I left at ten minutes of six but could not get a taxi at once." Freud said no more, and I began my analysis.

Apropos of some point, during the hour, Freud said,

44

"Perhaps you accepted some of the criticisms in the paper of Dr. Roback." (It was a paper on Freud's theories of slips, which Freud gave me to read.) "It was a silly paper," continued Freud. "I found him to be so inaccurate in his book that I accept nothing he says. The inaccuracies, to be sure, are of little consequence. He says, for example, that I could talk for only a half hour a day when I was ill. This is nonsense. I could talk all I wished to, as soon as I got my plate. And again, he makes the wife of Jones the sister of so-and-so." (I have forgotten the name.) "This is not true. She is the sister of X. And so on. He merely wrote what he thought, without checking up. When a man is so inaccurate in small matters, I take no interest in anything that he writes."

February 27, 1930

Yesterday Professor Freud talked for almost the whole hour. He asked me first about the dream that I was working on when we parted the previous hour. He said, "We were at a very interesting point in your dream, where you were talking about the decorations in the church."

The dream was about a Methodist preacher who had built a very compact but stupidly designed church. There is only one door, and the two steps leading up to it are so arranged that the lower one, when raised, is a stool for adults, while the higher step, when raised, is a stool for children. The walls have red and gold decorations like those at the museum I visited the day before. A veil is stretched over the ceiling, on which clouds are painted, and through it shine

45

lights resembling the sun and moon. The furniture is of golden oak. In the rear is a tank for immersion (this despite the church being a Methodist one). The tank has a small cast-iron bathtub, like a coffin, too small for immersion. One end is broken. The preacher shows us around.

Associations: The steps and the stool show my attitude toward analysis in the dream. The church is analysis. The dream is a criticism of anlaysis. Analysis deals too much with the anal aspects of life, especially with that of the child. The decorations: I said that psychoanalysis is a kind of religion but suited only to the very intelligent, for it would be very arid for the average person. So the decorations are put in to add richness to the religion of analysis.

"You see," Freud commented, "you can never tell what a thing means until you have associated to it." (This is too strong; he said "often" not "never.") "In one case, decorations might mean something else. The veil and the lights mean that analysis has taken away heaven. And the broken tank means circumcision. It is really a Jew that has built the house and is showing you about."

Next I expressed my belief that we could not always explain a man's profession by some simple compensation or sublimation, even though a man might, for example, become a surgeon because of a sublimation of a sadistic impulse.

"Of course," said Freud, "a man may be a surgeon through accident, but a really good surgeon is one who has made this fundamental sublimation.

"Do you know why psychiatrists go into their specialty?" he continued. "It is because they do not feel that they are normal, and they go into this work because it is a means of sublimation for this feeling—a means of assuring themselves that they are really normal. Society puts them in charge of the mentally abnormal, and so they feel reassured. Also, they are so much more normal than their patients. . . . Of course, some psychiatrists go into this work through accident."

As an example of this, Freud gave me the case of Dr. Wagner-Jauregg, who had tried in vain to get a position in all the different departments of the hospital. Not finding an opening, he was forced to go into psychiatry, where (being a very brilliant man) he made a great success. "He does not fulfill my theory," said Freud.

March 6, 1930

I had a wonderful hour with Professor Freud tonight. I spoke of my reading some articles in the *Collected Papers* on instincts and the unconscious, and said I felt I should memorize these papers.

Freud asked me whether I had read recently the *Three Contributions to the Theory of Sex*. I replied that I had read it some time ago.

"That was written in 1905," said Freud. "It is now more or less an historical document. It is necessary to make additions and subtractions—to take off some of the corners. I tried to make some changes in later editions but found that it was impossible. It is better to leave it as it is—an historical document."

"It is better, I suppose, to write a new book," I ventured.

"That will be for others to do," Freud replied. "In developing a new science," he continued, "one has to make its theories vague. You cannot make things clear-cut. But when you write, the public demands that you make things definite, else they think that you do not know what you are saying.

"Now, in the matter of papers on technique," he went on, "I feel that they are entirely inadequate. I do not believe that one can give the methods of technique through papers. It must be done by personal teaching. Of course, beginners probably need something to start with. Otherwise they would have nothing to go on. But if they follow the directions conscientiously, they will soon find themselves in trouble. Then they must learn to develop their own technique."

I owed the professor $150 for February. I get the dollars, which he prefers to shillings, from Thomas Cook, but I could not get the full amount on the 28th. So today I got all the money Cook had—$500. This enabled me to pay the $150 I owed. As I did not wish to keep the rest in my house, I gave the other $350 to Freud on account. As he took it, he said, "You must promise to ask for a return of this from my family in case of my premature death."

Once before, when I paid him $100 in advance, he had said the same thing. I asked him at that time if he had any reason to think that he might die suddenly.

"No special reason," he had replied. "The other day I went to the doctor about some irregularity of my heart. The doctor said, 'I don't know whether I can help you. When you have a small thing the matter, often you cannot do much about it. However, I am sure that the condition is not dangerous.' "

Freud then continued, "I think about the possibility of death every day. It is good practice."

DIARY OF MY ANALYSIS WITH SIGMUND FREUD

March 7, 1930

Yesterday, as I left, Freud said, "Perhaps you may have something more to say about your attitude toward analysis."

Last night, under this stimulus, I had two dreams. In the first, I am sitting in a chair and Freud is facing me. I am just talking. During the hour, a secretary comes into the room, a woman with many cards. Later, a man comes into the room with some manuscript. I feel that this is a very poor way to carry on an analysis. I feel I am not getting my money's worth.

In the second dream, I am about to make a speech about psychoanalysis and education. The crowd is waiting. Freud, dressed in a black suit, comes from out a rear room, and I realize that he is to hear my speech. Although he goes back into his room, I know that he can hear me, and I feel embarrassed about this.

Associations to second dream: Dr. Lippman* is having

---

*Dr. Hyman Lippman was a pediatrician friend of ours from Minnesota who also came over that year to study in Vienna. He lived on the same floor with us at the Pension Atlanta—as did another American friend, Dr. Edith Jackson, who was working with Freud—and we spent many long hours together "discussing." We were in fact part of a large American colony consisting of musicians, journalists, medical people studying in Vienna, and a large number who were studying analysis.

In a curious fashion, the whole of the foreign colony seemed to revolve around Freud—including, we felt, a certain type of maladjusted who came to be where they could misquote him most easily, and even give expression to their hatred of him. I recall, for example, that one of the leading journalists, Robert Best, turned out to be an important American Nazi who eventually died in a government prison in the States.

Freud himself rarely went out. When he did go, as to the annual song recital of his old friend Yvette Guilbert, it created a furore in his group of admirers and a mild excitement in all of intellectual Vienna. Amusingly enough, Guilbert played entirely to the professor, and the audience hardly saw Guilbert for watching him. But Freud did not seem conscious of the excitement he was creating, and his poise remained unshaken.—*M.G.B.*

49

talks with Dr. Nunberg. Lippman says it is the same as analysis, but I think that he is just fooling himself. This is not analysis. Then I speak of lying down. I say to Lippman that his lying down was but a technical device, that one could use a chair.

"Yes," commented Freud at this point, "the lying down is but a matter of convenience. But there is one point that is essential: the analysand must not see the face of the analyst. If he did, he would be influenced by the face of the analyst."

On the whole, the dream means that I repudiate analysis that is not carried on according to rule. Also, I have some doubts about my being able to present analysis in the best light.

During the discussion, Freud also said, "Perhaps you are too optimistic about getting analysis accepted. Take the word of an old man like me—analysis necessarily raises resistance. The fact that we have an unconscious means the presence of resistance. And you cannot present analysis in such a way as not to arouse resistances. It is only in analysis—with difficulty, with much patience, and with much repetition—that we can overcome this resistance."

Freud continued, "When Jung went to the United States, while he was my right-hand man, he wrote me that by modifying analysis in some respects he had overcome the resistances of the American audiences, I wrote back that this was too bad; you could overcome *all* the resistances by modifying analysis still more."

Speaking of Dr. Putnam of Harvard, Freud said, "His death was a great loss. I felt protected behind his personality as behind a shield. But he was too old when he accepted analysis. If he had lived, he would have advanced analysis a great deal more. His acceptance of analysis was almost a miracle."

March 20, 1930

I told Freud that I had been reading his article "A Child Is Being Beaten" and said, "I suppose that the sense of sin arises from the Oedipus complex at first, and then is transferred to the masturbatory activity."

"Yes," he replied, "but that is not the only way the sense of sin arises. When was the article written?"

"In 1910, I think."

"No," said Freud, "it must have been later," and he went to his library to look up the article. It proved to have been written in 1919. That led Freud to say, "May I make a suggestion: In reading articles about analysis, look at the date of the article. The *Zeitschrift* is a good magazine to read; here are the latest findings."

Continuing, he said, "Few of the formulations of psychoanalysis have been proved wrong, but many of them have to be amended. We still believe that the Oedipus complex is the center of the neurosis in men and in some cases in women. But in the last five years or so, we have found out that in some girls, their neurotic symptoms go back to a preoedipal stage. It is the attachment to the mother that is the cause of the neurosis or the neurotic tendency."

I asked, "In case the girl's attachment does not give rise to a homosexual reaction, what sort of neurosis does it give rise to?"

"To any kind of neurosis," replied Freud. "The woman

is most complicated. In the case of the boy, he becomes attached to his mother and remains attached. But in the case of the girl, she becomes attached to her mother and then must break away and become attached to her father. In the case of the girl, it is a broken line that her development follows. It is only in the last few years that we have begun to realize just how complicated is the development of the girl."

Referring to the necessity of checking the dates of the papers written on analysis, Freud remarked, "It is just this which the critics fail to do. They seem to think that analysis was dropped from heaven or erupted from hell—that it is fixed like a block of lava and not a body of facts which have been slowly and painfully gathered by scientific research."

March 26, 1930

Today Freud said, "You know that histology has found out that the sex organs of the newborn are highly developed, and this development either continues (or at least holds its own) for two or three years and then there is a regression. This was a striking confirmation from physiology of the findings of analysis. Ferenczi called our attention to this histological work. People had no idea of this childhood development of sex until analysis brought it out." He then added that "the young child has erections during the first few months."

I said, "Margaret has showed that the newborn have erections."

Freud was much interested, and wanted to know where this article was published.* Concerning stuttering, Freud said, "I know nothing about it, but it seems to me that the motive might be an oral eroticism, as Dr. Coriat said." (I had been discussing Coriat's book on stammering.) "But the mechanism is physiological. There must be some constitutional condition as well as the psychological motive."

Yesterday I gave four brief dreams. Freud commented, "It is best to make a brief survey of all the dreams, rather than try to work out one dream in too great detail."

March 30, 1930

A very interesting session today. Freud spoke much of the hour and took an active part in analyzing my dreams for me.

After discussing one of my dreams, he continued, "You know that boys, after they have been passive, always become active. For example, a boy just had a visit from the doctor, who opened the boy's mouth and looked in his throat. As soon as the doctor was gone, the boy tried to look in his sister's throat. Boys always take an active role after they have had to take a passive role."

Speaking about the double standard, Freud said, "It has been my experience that when women have a love affair, they are absolutely lost to analysis. I do not know if American women have so far advanced in their virility striving as to be able to have an affair with no more reaction than a

*"The Behavior of the Human Infant During the First 30 Days of Life," *Psychological Review*, Vol. XXIV, No. 6 (November, 1917).

man. In the case of a man, he seems to be able to have an affair without such a complete immersion. He has other interests. He can go on with his treatment."

April 4, 1930

As we began the session today, Freud said, "You must follow the rule of analysis and be free to let your mind go as it will. Do not feel that you must keep along some preconceived path. You will probably get where you are going just the same. The analyst must follow where you go."

I asked, "Do you think we dream whether we remember them or not?"

"It depends on what you mean by dreaming," he replied. "If you mean the result of the dream work, then you must remember it, to have dreamed."

"But," I said, "does the unconscious have the outlets from its tensions and wishes whether you remember them or not?"

"The unconscious does not have tensions or wishes," he answered. "It is the conscious mind that has these tensions. The dream is to relieve these."

I must ask about this again. I am afraid I did not understand him.

Today I met Freud's maid, Paula—a sweet, timid, eager girl of about 21—in Dr. Steiner's office, and I began to talk to her. I wanted to get her impression of Freud. She said, *"Doktor Freud ist sehr sympathetisch, und gut und nett"* (sympathetic and kind and nice). It was interesting to get the maid's impression of Freud's character.

Today, as I left, Freud gave me the March, 1930, issue

of the *Medical Review of Reviews,* which was a symposium on psychopathology, with an introduction by himself. It was an example of his thoughtfulness. "I thought you might like to just look this over," he said. "Don't take the trouble to read it."

Three days ago, referring to a previous discussion, Freud said to me, "I have the impression, now that you have found out about the Canadian girl, that you feel you need not probe deeper but can keep to general principles.

"This is the most sophisticated kind of resistance. I remember a case of a woman who came to me from Prague when I was just beginning analysis. (Of course, at that time I made many foolish mistakes.) She spent the hour telling me how happy she was with her husband. At the end of the hour I told her that I did not believe this possible, that I never saw a woman who had a neurosis who was happy in her married life. Today, I should let the patient talk and say nothing. But then I was not so experienced. The next day the woman came back and said, 'All you told me was quite true. I see that you were right, and now I am quite well and have no more need of treatment.' And she went home.

"Two weeks later, I heard that she had had to go to a sanatorium. She had said she was getting along all right in order to keep from having to talk about her difficulties. This mechanism is used not infrequently."

April 19, 1930

Earlier this week, Freud suggested as a piece of active therapy that I try to sleep on my back or side. My custom since childhood is to sleep on my stomach, with one leg drawn up. Freud said this position of mine was probably derived from some childish, or rather infantile, experience.

The last two nights Freud has had his chow dog in the room. Two nights ago, as he came out of his hour with Dr. Jackson, he ran through the hall like a boy, expecting the dog to follow. But Dr. Jackson (she was just leaving) spoke to the dog, and the dog remained to speak to her.

Last night I dreamed that Bobs, my dog, found a porcupine in a hollow tree. He flung the porcupine out. At first I thought it was a coon. Then Bobs swallowed the porcupine. I cut it out of Bobs' throat, but in so doing I got some quills in my thumb.

Associations: The night before, Dr. Lippman had been telling us about a baby that had cried for hours. The mother brought the child to him, but he could find nothing. Finally the mother called his attention to the baby's swollen thumb. I also remembered that babies were said to come from hollow stumps, and I thought of the "fretful porcupine" [*sic*], a quotation from *Hamlet*. During today's session I recalled another Shakespeare quotation—"untimely rippèd from his mother's womb"—which I said was from *Julius Caesar*.

"No," corrected Freud, "it was said of Macduff in *Macbeth*."

This is an example of Freud's erudition and wide reading. Imagine an American doctor knowing some little quotation from Schiller or Goethe!

Mention of the porcupine led Freud to say, "When I was asked to go to America in 1909, I did not expect much, but I wanted to see a porcupine. In the Adirondacks, I saw a dead one. When I got back, Dr. Ferenczi gave me this little model." Whereupon he went into his room and brought out a small model of a porcupine for me to see. We spoke of its habits, then went on with the associations to my dream.

April 23, 1930*

Today was the first time I had seen Freud since April 19. (I have been to Budapest for a visit. Saw Dr. Ferenczi, who was much interested in the problem of stuttering. He thinks we should analyze some cases and see what we get.)

During today's session, I mentioned some clippings I had seen about Freud's new book, *Civilization and Its Discontents.* One was by a preacher who said that Freud was drenched in despair and gloom. Another was an editorial criticizing Freud for saying that primitive man was happy and uninhibited.

Freud said, "The English translation is not yet out—how can they know what the book says? They review it from reports that they have received, without reading the book."

I then spoke of Dr. A's negative transference to Ferenczi. Later I spoke of my transference to Freud as not being negative.

"There is just one thing—perhaps I should not mention it," Freud remarked, "but I will give it to you for what it

*Freud had to suspend the analysis after April 23 because of personal health problems requiring urgent attention. On April 24 he went to the Cottage Sanatorium in Vienna for treatment of his cardiac condition. He remained there until May 4, when he went to Berlin to have a new prosthesis made, for the old one had again been causing him great distress. He stayed as usual at the sanatorium in Tegel, where he had to remain for several months before the dental work was completed. Smiley went to Berlin to continue his sessions with Freud, but apparently the meetings were very irregular, and there are no diary entries for this period other than the final one in June.—*M.G.B.*

is worth. Perhaps you have not been entirely frank. It sometimes happens that a patient makes a mental reservation, which is easy to do, and then the analysis goes on happily and smoothly, with little or no negative transference."

I asked Freud if there was any direct evidence of this in my case.

"No," he replied, "I only gave it as a possibility. Perhaps the one thing I might mention is the optimistic attitude toward persons and things that you often take."

Then I asked Freud about the question I had discussed with Margaret and Hy Lippman—about a person making a reservation, such as a priest.

"I will give you an example," he replied. "Before the war, a man came to me for analysis. He said he had a nervous difficulty: He felt nervous and confused in the presence of those in high authority. He was in the diplomatic service. He was Hungarian and had been called to be private secretary to the Emperor. Before facing his superiors, he always had to take alcohol, and he did not wish to continue this practice. He also said that he was required to swear not to reveal the secrets of his work to anyone.

"I consented to try to help him. But I found that he blocked behind his reservations, and although I treated him for nine months—and he was satisfied, was partially relieved of his symptoms, and even still speaks of the benefits of his treatment—I do not feel that it was a satisfactory analysis."

I asked Freud what he thought of my studying with Dr. Brill when I got back to New York—of having him help me with my analytic work.

Freud said that would be fine. "Brill is very fine—none better."

DIARY OF MY ANALYSIS WITH SIGMUND FREUD

June, 1930

I visited with Freud a few minutes on my last day at Tegel. He gave me a letter of introduction to Dr. Ernest Jones, whom I expect to visit in London on my way back home.*

Freud asked me what my plans were, and I told him I had decided to work with Dr. Brill after I got back.

"Do you think," I asked, "that after working with Dr. Brill for a year I will be ready to practice analysis?"

"Yes," Freud replied, "I think you have the groundwork so you can go ahead." Then he volunteered, "I don't think you are neurotic."

*Smiley had to return to Vassar to teach in the summer school. I also had to return to give summer classes in child guidance, but I waited a few weeks longer before doing so. Then, early in September, I returned alone to Vienna to continue my analysis with Dr. Brunswick, while Smiley remained at Vassar for the regular school year.

It was during the following spring in Vienna that I met Freud again. I was living, at the time, with the family of an artist at No. 1, Frankgasse. One day, as I was going down the marble stairs to the street floor, I saw, on the landing below, a very weary and crumpled-looking little old man accompanied by a younger man in a chauffeur's cap. I looked again—and saw something about him that was neither little nor weary nor old. Even his simplest movements had a distinguished, controlled simplicity. Another glance told me it was the professor. Then I recalled that the office of his oral surgeon was in that building.

On the ground floor we drew abreast of one another. I hesitated to intrude, yet I could not very well pass by without a brief greeting. "Good morning, professor," I said.

He glanced up and stopped. Then, extending his hand, he exclaimed, "Smiley's Margaret!" and laughingly led me to a better light, where he studied my face under the broad brim of my straw hat.

"Well, well," he said, "I have often recommended analysis in order to make people happier, but I did not realize that it might also make them younger!"

After a question or two as to what news I had of Smiley from New York and how I found life in Vienna, he smilingly departed.

He must have been utterly weary and quite spent with pain at that moment, but if so, he laid that aside for the kindly greeting and the very Viennese compliment: the courteous little gesture that endeavors always to make the other person, and not one's self, the center of the stage. At least, that was Vienna before the fall!—M.G.B.

There were a few final words, and then, shaking hands, we parted.

VIENNA

August 3, 1935

I called Freud's house in Grinzing* last evening after arriving by plane from London at 8 P.M. Anna Freud was out. At 10 she was still out, and I did not reach her until 9 o'clock this morning. She gave me an appointment with her father at 4 P.M.

The house is at 47 Strassergasse. I left Pension Atlanta by the car line at 2:45 to be sure to be on time. As I was approaching the house, about 3:10, I saw Anna Freud leaving in her automobile with Paula, the little maid I had last seen five years ago. Fraulein Freud stopped and spoke to me cordially, and suggested that I sit in the garden at the rear of the house. I asked if I must ring the gate bell—which I did—but the maid came from the car and took me to the rear. She said I could stay there until 4, when I would be sent for.

The garden is about 50 yards wide and 100 deep, with many trees and soft, warm grass. After exploring the garden to its end, I seated myself at a table in a comfortable chair

*A suburb of Vienna, where Freud was spending the summer.

and waited. The birds chirped and sang; there was a soft breeze. The maids occasionally talked loudly in the kitchen in the front of the house, which is of cream-colored stucco. It has three stories with French windows, and there is a porch on the west end of it where Professor Freud was.

As the clock struck four, the maid who had let me in returned and asked me to follow her. I went up the outside stairs to the porch, some ten feet high. At the far end on a couch, dressed in his usual pepper-and-salt suit, lay Professer Freud.

He held out his hand but did not rise. "How are you?" he said, and then asked about Margaret. He motioned me to draw my chair nearer. He seemed very frail but keen and alert. After an exchange of the amenities, he said, "I shall not see you today for a regular appointment. To be frank, I am not feeling well. My doctor says my heart is not strong. It's nothing; but he says I had best not work today."

In reply to his next question, I said I intended to stay two weeks at least—that would give us 12 hours—and perhaps a few days more if I could. I then told him I had brought the fee for two weeks in dollars—thinking perhaps he would prefer this as he had done five years before.

"It's of no importance," he said, whereupon I asked him to accept the $300 (which I had with me in three 100-dollar bills), as I did not want to carry it with me.

"I will accept it on account, and keep it for you. If I should die before the two weeks are over, it can be returned to you!

"You look the same," he then said. "It's been three years since I saw you."

"Five," I replied. "It was in 1930 when I left here."

"So it was," he said.

61

"Much water has passed under the bridge, and not all of it clear," I commented.

"Ah, yes," he agreed, with a weary shrug. Then he asked how it went with me.

I replied that I remained well despite five years of strenuous work, that I hoped I was wiser, and, I continued, "I am happier since my analysis."

"Did it help you *personally?*" he asked.

"Yes," I replied, "I think it was the most helpful thing —as far as personal understanding—that ever happened to me."

He impulsively held out his hand, which I grasped. It was a genuine show of feeling on his part, unusual and spontaneous.

"I think of you often and with the deepest affection," I continued, "even though you do not hear from me often."

(I forgot to note before that when he spoke of his heart, I had offered to leave, but he said he could talk without difficulty.)

Freud then said I could have either 11 A.M. or 4 P.M. He was seeing only one other person, for everyone was away on holiday. I said I would prefer the 11 o'clock hour.

"That is all right," he replied. "Then I shall see you Monday at 12 o'clock."

"Eleven," I said.

"Ah, yes," he replied and held out his hand.

The visit lasted about twelve minutes.

Freud gave me the impression of mental alertness, of an energy of spirit and a keen command of the situation. He did not seem weak but very frail and rather thin. His movements were quick and even birdlike in their suddenness— for example, in putting out his hand. His mind moved swiftly. Apparently he was a bit hard of hearing—or perhaps he was not accustomed to my English. Once or twice he asked me to repeat a sentence, especially in discussing Margaret's health.

I told him that we had just written another book about stutterers which has been accepted for publication. "You have written another book?" he said with interest. "You collaborate?"

"Yes," I replied.

August 5, 1935

I arrived at Freud's house a few minutes before 11 o'clock. The gate was unlocked for me and the little maid, Paula, came down the path to meet me. This time I was shown into a room which opened on the porch where Freud had been lying on Saturday. The professor was in the middle of the room—looking quite fit and energetic. He shook hands and waved me to the couch.

"You have not changed," I said. He did not reply but made the customary grunt in his throat to indicate agreement. "Your energy and spirit," I went on, "continue to push forward." He did not reply.

I then said, "I did not inquire if your fee was the same as before. I assumed it—but if it is more because of the value of dollars, let me know, and I shall arrange to make up the difference."

"It is quite all right," he replied. Then he added, "Is it convenient for you to pay me the sum you gave me?" The tone of his voice and the implication of his manner was plainly that he would reduce the fee if I could not afford the usual sum of $25 an hour.

"Yes," I replied, "I saved the sum for this purpose. I had to effect some economies to do so, but unless one makes some sacrifice, one does not appreciate things."

I settled back, and began, "First, I shall tell you of my objective life, then of my subjective life briefly since I left you." He replied, "Whatever you like."

I spoke of my meeting with Zilboorg. "Oh, yes," said Freud, "a newcomer."

Continuing, I said I felt that there was a movement on foot to oust Dr. Brill. Freud remarked, "After all, he seems to be the best."

"Undoubtedly," I replied. "He is often somewhat tactless and lacking in social finesse at the meetings, but he has been very kind to me and I am his firm supporter."

I spoke of Y's analysis and of his killing the woman. Freud said nothing. I spoke of Kardiner's and Zilboorg's opposition to me, and of my opinion of them. Again there was no comment.

I had to speak quite loudly and slowly. Apparently Freud is now slightly deaf. His speech was not quite distinct, his tone was low-pitched, and it seemed difficult for him to get the energy to articulate.

Again one is impressed by Freud's ability to be aloof yet at the same time gracious and warm and friendly. His expression of agreement by an indefinite exclamation gives the patient the impression that he is being listened to with great attention (which is the case) and that what he says is important and in agreement with the professor's views. He has learned the difficult art of the countertransference. He gives of himself—but not indiscriminately or in a way that would burden the patient with the necessity of returning affection for affection, of like for like. . . . His handshake is somewhat limp: his hand hangs down from his arm. His movements, as always, are quick and birdlike—almost feminine in their quickness and delicacy.

August 6, 1935

Today I began by talking about Dr. Alexander's sister. (Margaret had just written me about meeting her at Clara's.) Freud did not know her.

Of one of Ferenczi's pupils, Freud said, "She had, I'm afraid, a bad influence on Ferenczi." Of Dr. Horney, he said, "She is able but malicious—mean."

I spoke of Dr. X's apparent homosexuality (overt) and of his relation to Dr. Y., who sends him patients. I said, "I do not feel an overt homosexual would make a good analyst." Freud's reply, in effect, was "You are right in your assumption."

I then gave a detailed history again of Mrs. Y. Several times I paused after asking a question, such as "Do you think her father means this to her?" There was silence after these questions. At one point I remarked, "Mrs. Y. seems to have an anal penis. . . . Perhaps all little girls do, when they feel they have not a real penis."

Freud replied, "The sensation in the clitoris has more influence in shaping the attitudes than the size of the stool which is experienced on evacuation." (These are not his exact words but convey his meaning.)

Finally Freud said, "It seems as though you wish to have me work with you as though I were controlling you in your analysis. In a control, you start in the first week and get your impression of the patient—and the next week, and so on. But to enter into a case which has been going on for so long, and whose history is so involved, is impossible. You cannot get an adequate opinion."

I nevertheless gave three of Mrs. Y's dreams; but to my questions about them there was either silence or a statement that without the associations no opinion could be given.

I asked if it was good technique to bring a patient back to a dream. "Yes," he replied, "but if the patient will not go ahead, you can do nothing. You cannot push things. You give me the impression of trying too hard. Your interests could be better directed, perhaps, to attention to the method. Do your work as thoroughly as you can, and do not worry about the results. Do not give yourself too much trouble." He then quoted the motto on Paré's tomb, giving it in French. I asked him to translate it. "You cannot understand my French?" he asked. I replied, "I cannot understand anyone's French, I am sorry to say." Whereupon he gave the translation: "I treated (bandaged) my patients—God cured them."

Earlier, in speaking of Mrs. D's symptoms, including her rejection of the sensations of the vagina, I said, "I presume I must not expect to solve the patient's sexual frigidity and give her sexual response."

"No," Freud replied, "you must not be too ambitious."

I asked if one might expect to help Mr. L., aged 26 or 27, to achieve sexual potency.

"Yes," said Freud. "One may look for results at such an age. I had a man of 35 who achieved sexual potency after treatment."

August 7, 1935

During the hour there was a rattling of the door. Freud got up, opened it, and his chow dog came in.

While [I was] analyzing my dreams, the name of Ferenczi came up again, and I asked Freud what was the kernel of his new idea. Freud's reply, in essence, was this:

"You cannot understand Ferenczi's method without understanding his whole history. He was one of eleven children. His mother was intelligent and efficient, but naturally she could not give this child much love. He could not be singled out. He was starved for love. That was his secret, which came out when he was being analyzed by me.

"His 'new method'—it had nothing to do with his active therapy, which, by the way, worked very well—was really a passive surrender to the patient. His idea was to satisfy the infantile wishes of the patient and thus get at the infantile material at an earlier and more plastic stage.

"I asked him," continued Freud, "if he were getting results. 'No, not yet,' he said, but he expected to. Now, if a father were to surrender to every wish of his young child, it would be impossible to have any adequate training. The father must train the child. The analyst, also, cannot surrender to the infantile wishes of his patient. Ferenczi tried to play the part of an overtender father, to give the love he himself had not received and to get love from his patients. That was his secret. He was ill for several years before his death. And during this illness, this tendency to give and get love, because of his childhood starved condition, came out."

I asked Freud what he would do if a patient insisted on

sitting up, or on using a powder puff and making up during analysis. "I should not permit it," he replied. "I should say, 'You are putting yourself out of the analytic situation.'"

Later I asked him, "Would you continue, on the second or succeeding days, analyzing a dream?"

"Yes," he replied, "unless a new dream came, and then I should generally leave the old dream and start with the new one. . . . But you realize," he added, "that when a patient brings you a new dream when they have not analyzed the old dream, it means resistance."

To a question about his children, Freud said he had three sons, all of whom had had to leave Germany. One was an architect in London, one an engineer in France, and the other an attorney here in Vienna.

"No Jew," I said, "can expect justice in Germany, so they should leave there if they can." Freud agreed.

In the course of the associations to my dream, Freud said, "I get the impression that you were disappointed and dissatisfied, that you wanted to leave before your time, that you wanted to be a member of my family."

August 8, 1935

I came with a dream but had difficulty finding its meaning.

"You seem to be holding back something," said Freud. "It is better not to prepare what you are to say. Come in a more passive attitude." He added that there was something different in my voice; he could not understand me so well. Also, I covered my eyes, and he wondered what this meant. I explained that my eyes hurt me. He also questioned my looking at my watch so often last time. Perhaps it meant that I was bored or that I felt he was not giving me a full hour. On the contrary, I told him, the last hour was most interesting, but my watch had stopped just forty minutes after the hour.

"You see how difficult it is for me to understand the meaning of things unless I have the associations," he commented. "They may have so many meanings."

Finally, at the end of the hour, Freud said that in my dream, apparently, the university chancellor was also he, Freud, and that my wish for the chancellor to live was probably a contradictory wish against the death wish.

I said, "Probably one of the reasons for my resistance was an embarrassing question I wanted to ask you. At sixty-five, I expect to write my autobiography and put down frankly what impress American civilization has made on me. I shall want to use material you have said to me and my impressions of you. This is the embarrassing question I have to ask."

Freud asked me why I should wait until I was sixty-five to write my autobiography. I replied that it might offend people, and I wanted to wait until I was able to retire.

He then said, "I don't see why the question was embarrassing. You have your personal relations with me, and you are free to write what you like."

I replied, "So many people who have known you (like Wittels, for example) have made—I can't think of the word."

"Made a mess," Freud interpolated.

"Yes," I said, "but that is not the word." Finally it came to me: "Made capital out of you."

"Ah," he said, but then repeated, "but you are free to write what you like."

August 9, 1935

I had several weird dreams during the night and slept poorly. I arrived about ten minutes early for the session, and found Frau Freud sitting at the garden table, cutting beans efficiently in small pieces for the dinner meal. She is a well-rounded, matronly woman of medium size, and about 5'2" tall, I should judge. She has a sweet mouth and a gracious, kindly expression. She seemed quite timid. I remarked that I was early and that the garden was *"ruhig und schön."* She replied with a smile and a nod but did not speak. The maid came about five minutes before the hour to call me. Probably the professor wished to avoid embarrassing Frau Freud. I shall arrive, hereafter, just on time.

Freud had said that when a person brings a new dream before having analyzed the old one, it means a resistance. When I told him that I had brought several dreams, he said, "Well, take the one that made the greatest impression on you."

The dream included episodes about an animal like a deer or antelope with coarse brown fur, and the associations brought up Anna's dog and the professor's own dog.

During the hour, someone knocked at the door. It was Ettinger, to say good-bye. When the knock came, Freud's chow barked, and after Ettinger left, the professor said proudly, "You see how she keeps watch." This led me to recall the episode in 1929, when I asked that the dog be taken out of the room while I was being analyzed.

"It was not this dog, was it?" asked Freud.

"No, it was Anna's dog," I replied.

"Oh . . . Wolf," he said, as though it was a slur on his

dog to say she interfered with the analysis. The chow, in fact, usually lies quietly on the floor. Once, when she was gnawing a bone loudly, Freud asked her to stop, which she promptly did. The other day, however, she was outside and had growled at me when I left. I mentioned this to Freud.

"Growled at you?" he repeated, as though astonished that his dog could do such a thing.

I said, "Yes—Saturday as I left, before she knew me."

Among the associations to the dream, I spoke of Graves's books *I, Claudius* and *Claudius the God*. Freud, who had read them both, agreed that Caligula had an attack of catatonic dementia praecox and that Claudius was a case of Little's disease (birth injury), about which he had written a monograph before he took up analysis. He agreed that Claudius' injury left his intellect unimpaired but offered one criticism that might be brought against Graves. The writers of this period (some of them republicans) who tell of the Emperor's doings were unfriendly and doubtless were not correct reporters of the situation. For instance, Livia may not have been a "mean witch" at all.

In a discussion about technique, I asked Freud if he advocated talking to a patient several hours before analysis—or, rather, to begin an analysis with several hours of discussion.

He replied, "With a student in training, it may be permissible. With a patient who is there for treatment, no."

I asked him about P. and his wearing of women's underclothes. Freud agreed that it was a mother identification toward his father, yet it may be that he does not differentiate between the sexes—his fantasies, Freud went on to say, must be treated with caution. They are often so distorted in such cases as to cover the more primitive reactions.

I asked Freud if he had written his *Interpretation of Dreams* in one summer. "The first draft," he replied. "Of course, much had to be left for a later revision."

"It was a remarkable tour de force," I said. "The more I read the book, the more remarkable it becomes. . . . And," I continued, "you are so sure—that is, your touch is so certain—there is no fiddling about. You do not hesitate to say, 'Dreams are always such or such.' "

"Perhaps," he replied, "my sureness was due to the enthusiasm of the young discoverer."

August 10, 1935

Saturday was not a successful day, it seemed. I slept poorly. I moved to the Bristol Hotel Friday night but found it noisy and moved back to Pension Atlanta. The professor seemed a little bored or tired. Perhaps it was my attitude.

I spoke of P. and tried to get at the mechanism by which homosexuality is arrived at. Freud said, "When a mother is too tender with her child—that is, boy child—homosexuality often develops." I judge he meant as a defense against the incestuous feelings.

I next spoke of Mr. W., of my failure to see his growing transference and his anger—his paranoid anger against me. I said, "I was a little shocked at the closely knit paranoid structure he had built up—one that I could not break through. . . . I often wonder," I went on, "if my reasoning is so warped." There was no sign from the professor.

Still discussing Mr. W's attitude, I said, "A man's homosexual attitude is not necessarily a feminine characteristic, but it is an infantile attitude." Margaret had made this suggestion, and I said I concurred. Freud commented, "Well, in some cases that may be so, but it does not seem to be of universal application."

When I said Mr. W. had announced that he would not return, Freud made an exclamation—but I hastened to add that he did return. Later, Freud spoke of P. as being a case of infantilism, of not having grown up. But he gave me no encouragement when I said I felt I had been unwise with Mr. W. He only said, "The mechanism of homosexuality is not clear."

Finally, in speaking of the 1st Presbyterian Church of New Rochelle and its pastor, with whom I had discussed Bible reading, I mentioned that I had won $5 from a friend on my Bible knowledge. I went on, "It is usually thought that Ruth's statement, 'Intreat me not to leave thee,' etc., was said to her husband, but really it was said to her mother-in-law."

Freud said he thought it was to her husband. I repeated that it was not. "I'll have to look it up," he said.

I forgot to note the other day that when we were discussing the Treaty of Versailles and Wilson, I remarked that Wilson was skinned (outwitted) by Lloyd George and Clemenceau.

Freud replied, "Wilson was absolutely ignorant."

August 12, 1935

I asked Freud about his new ideas on anxiety, as suggested in a footnote in my copy of the *Interpretation of Dreams.*

"You know," he replied, "our ideas about anxiety have changed a great deal since this book was written. You will find the new ideas in a chapter in the *New Introductory Lectures on Psychoanalysis.*"

I then told the professor about our findings and theories about stuttering. At the end of a 15-minute exposition, I said, "Our findings are that there are two types of stuttering: one in which the organism is involved and one in which speech is involved." And I gave examples.

Freud expressed neither agreement nor disagreement. I felt he was not impressed with our two types. I went on to say that we had found in our cases an accentuation of the anal erotic impulses which was transferred to the oral erotic area. There was a passive homosexual tendency and a castration feeling. But, I said, we did not wish to generalize from these few cases. And I told him a story about a friend of mine, a negative-minded fellow, with whom I had been walking one day on the university farm. As we passed a field where some newly shorn sheep were grazing, I said, "I see they have sheared the sheep."

"Well," replied my friend, "on one side, at least." That was as far as he would go.

Freud laughed heartily. "Very good," he commented. He then said (in effect), "I have not had much experience with stutterers. One case was that of a man named Arthur. He began when he was 14 to stutter. He would say, 'Ah! Ah!'—which in German means to go to the toilet. This was a case of anal erotic origin. I am not sure of the passive homosexual side which you mention. It seems there are two divergent impulses. I am sure there are probably many different mechanisms in different cases."

I asked him if he still felt as he did about the organic factors in stuttering. "Yes," he replied. "There must be some bodily tendency." (He used a long German word which means bodily tendency or preparation.) "For, in one case we get asthma, in another, tics . . . and so on."

He did not seem to agree when I spoke of basal ganglion types.

August 13, 1935

I felt very tired yesterday afternoon. After sleeping for an hour and a half, I went downtown. I felt a very definite malaise. My legs were heavy, I had hot flashes, and I felt cold and sweaty hot—I felt really sick. The only physical explanation was a slight sinus infection I got swimming last Sunday.

When I spoke of this to the professor, he said, "Probably emotional—yesterday was a mild day—and then, too, these days make one tired."

I related last night's dream, which involved the Prince of Wales, Queen Victoria, and her inability to hear me when I addressed her, either because she is deaf or because my poor speech is at fault. I lean over a balcony rail and cry out to her, "You are still mistress of your realm, and you can still rule it despite your deafness."

It turned out, of course, that I equated Queen Victoria with Freud, and the professor was very amused by the dream. "Oh," he said, "I am a little hard of hearing, but if you speak a little slowly and a little louder—not yell—I can get it all."

There were other aspects to the dream, but I got nowhere with them. At the end of the hour, Freud said, "There is still some secret which we have not yet reached."

I forgot to make a note, the other day, about telling Freud that Margaret thought some of the prejudice against Jews was due to the fear created by them in the Gentiles through circumcision. I said I did not agree and asked if he did. He said no.

August 14, 1935

I asked the professor if it were permissible, when patients showed much resistance by saying they were getting nothing out of analysis and continued in that vein, to ask them what they expected from analysis and what were the difficulties they wish to understand or remove.

He replied, "Why not?"

We again discussed the Queen Victoria dream. It was brought out that I equated Queen Victoria with my grandmother also—and so the present Prince of Wales was I, since Victoria was his grandmother. My grandmother in reality was my mother as well, for she had reared me from an early age. We discussed aspects of homosexuality and the relation of my grandmother to the professor, whom I had turned into a woman (Victoria).

Later I brought up other questions on technique. At the end of the hour, Freud said, "You are perhaps too anxious about your patients." Then he added, in effect, "You must let them drift. Let them work out their own salvation." He quoted a butler in a play who said over and over, "It's no matter—it will work itself out."

August 15, 1935

I felt rather peaceful today. I asked the professor about Mrs. G. He said she seemed to be a good case for analysis—that her attachment for her father probably went back to her mother relationship. It would be necessary to analyze her homosexual relations to her mother to discover the reason for her father attachment.

I then spoke of my mother's strong will and the resolution with which she became a teacher in a society where women were not supposed to work . . . of my grandmother and her love, of her old-fashioned, rigid discipline, of her drinking during the final, senile year of her life, although she had always been a teetotaler. I spoke of her stubbornness—and also of the professor's in not coming to the U. S. for dental treatment.

Freud then asked my opinion of the dean of the Harvard dental school, but I did not know the man, although he had a reputation, apparently, as an expert. It seems he was in Paris several years ago, and Dr. Ruth Brunswick, Freud's devoted friend, had prevailed on him to come and examine the professor.

"He spent three weeks fixing my plate and charged $6,000," said Freud, "and it was not better than before."

I said the charge was outrageous. Freud could not remember the man's name but said he was considered one of the best for dental plates in the U. S. I replied that I doubted it very much.

I then spoke of the Jewish people—a few Semitic tribes, at the crossroads of the world, who developed a monotheism, a system of ethics, a god which all Europe accepted and yet hated the Jews for it—another miracle. . . . The professor made an exclamation to express his agreement with me.

I continued, "Speaking in sober judgment, I think you have one of the greatest minds of the ages. At the present day, you and perhaps Einstein are the two greatest minds in the world—and both Jewish."

Later, I got on the subject of America. On an earlier occasion, Freud had been critical of the country, referring to its poor education and culture. I cannot quote him exactly, but as nearly as I can remember it, he had said, "You Americans are like this: Garlic's good, chocolate's good—let's put a little garlic on chocolate and eat it."

I reminded him of this and then said, "I don't think you are fair to Americans. You must remember we are a democracy. The butler's and baker's sons go to college. In England and in Europe, you have an aristocracy of brains who get higher education. But we are free, and we have a free idealism. And it is my belief that psychoanalysis will find its best soil and growth in the U. S.—or at least among the 275 million English-speaking people. For I believe that the English-speaking people and probably the Russians will determine the future civilization."

To my optimistic view of psychoanalysis in the U. S., Freud replied, "I should die happy if I thought so, but I can see no sign of it now. It is rather being abused in the United States."

I admitted this but voiced the belief that in the future we should see a change. . . . "But why do I say all this?" I interrupted myself.

"It seems to be a sort of exhibitionism," replied Freud.

I went on to speak of how our Supreme Court protects the rights of the citizens—citing the new trial being given the Negroes in the Scottsboro case. I mentioned how Cardozo had been unanimously recommended by the New York Bar Association for the Supreme Court—and that of the nine men on this most powerful judicial body, two were Jews.

"Is that better than Queen Victoria taking a Jew for her prime minister?" said Freud.

"No," I conceded. "The British are as democratic as any country in the world." .

I felt somewhat discouraged after my hour, as though I had been childish and had showed off before the professor. When I said this to Freud, he replied, "Yes—but I am sure there must be some deeper reason."

I forgot to note something Freud said the other day when I asked him if it were not difficult to analyze Dr. Brunswick's husband, in view of the professor's previous social relations with him.

"It makes the analysis more difficult," replied Freud, "but this may be overcome. The Brunswicks have been friends of ours for ten years."

I also asked him if brother and sister, or husband and wife, might be analyzed at the same time. He replied that it is more difficult, to be sure, but sometimes it is necessary to do it.

August 17, 1935

Today was muggy. I walked out to Grinzing and had to hurry to get there on time. It had rained yesterday, and the little maid had given me an umbrella to get to the car line. I had a hard time remembering to bring it back, but I did and returned it to her when she came to announce me to the professor. As usual, he was standing in the middle of the room. As usual, too, he came forward and gave my hand a shake. Sometimes he only caught the end of my fingers, so quick and birdlike are his movements.

I sat on the couch and asked him if he would sign a copy of his *Interpretation of Dreams* for me—the one I had been studying. "If, however, it is your custom not to do this," I added, "I shall understand."

"Why not—for you?" he replied. He took the book, crossed over to his desk, and looked at the volume for a moment or two, leafing through some of the pages. Then he wrote carefully and slowly two lines in German which, translated, read:

To my dear Dr. Smiley Blanton
17-8-1935—for memory's sake.

I spent some time trying to analyze three recent dreams. They all seemed to represent childish wishes for love from the professor—to be passive in relation to him as my leader—and also to express my active heterosexual aspects.

Freud agreed with me concerning these wishes.

I then asked if it would not be wise to continue my analysis through self-analysis of dreams. "Yes," he said, "that is a way you can continue your analysis."

I said, "I seem to have no fundamental neurosis and no fundamental defect that will keep me from practicing analysis successfully." He made an exclamation that gave assent. Then I continued, "I did not get what I expected, which was advice about analysis and patients. But I got something better—a better knowledge of myself and a help in analyzing dreams." Again the professor made an assenting sound.

In the analysis of the last dream, I identified myself with the dog: A person was taking me away, but I wished to stay.

At last I said, "This is the end. I have a dim hope I may be able to return next summer—that I can get enough money to do it, if you could see me."

Freud replied, "I am sorry that I cannot promise to wait for you."

"Your health seems very good," I said. "I hope the difficulties in the world"—he understood that I meant the Jewish persecution—"will not distress you too much and make you too unhappy. There comes to my mind the line from a Latin poet whose name I have forgotten: 'Though the whole round world be overturned, let us still be undismayed.' "

Freud immediately identified the poet as Horace and quoted the Latin, adding, "It means 'Let us accept what comes'—or, as we would say it in slang, 'We can take it on the chin.' "

I got up. He gave me his hand, which I clasped.

"Good-bye," he said, adding, "Give my love to your wife."

"This will give her much pleasure," I replied. "Good-bye." As I went out, he turned away to his desk.

I left from the garden on the rear side of the house and came around to the street gate. It was unlatched, so I stepped out and turned to close it. To my surprise, I saw Freud standing at one of the windows of the consultation room that looks on the street. The house is about forty feet from the street. As I looked up, he waved to me good-bye. I waved back and took off my hat. I closed the gate, and when I looked again, he was gone.

As I walked down the narrow street of the oldtime village of Grinzing, the picture was indelibly etched on my mind of the frail, slight man with the fine, high forehead, the gray beard and white hair—waving good-bye. I must say my eyes remained misty for a little time.

NOTE: 1937

Smiley's practice had grown substantially by 1937, and his future career as an analyst was now assured. Our main summer project that year was a planned trip to Lourdes for the purpose of studying the nature and validity of the astonishing cures reported from its famous shrine. Smiley made a careful investigation along medical and psychiatric lines, and later published a monograph on his findings. I wrote a life of Bernadette entitled *Bernadette of Lourdes* which was published by Longmans, Green in 1939 and republished as *The Miracle of Lourdes* by Prentice-Hall in 1962.

The trip to Lourdes was scheduled for the latter part of August. Since we already planned to be in Europe, Smiley felt he would like to put in some further studies with Freud if that could be worked into our travel schedule. The professor, who was spending the summer again at Grinzing, fortunately had time available for Smiley at the beginning of August, and at the end of July we found ourselves once more in Vienna.

—M.G.B.

Vienna, Sunday, August 1, 1937

Margaret and I arrived in Vienna last Friday afternoon from Paris via the Orient Express. A rough ride, especially through France, the German railroad being much smoother.

Anna Freud answered when I called Freud's residence at seven in the evening. After checking with the professor, she gave me an appointment for five on Saturday. She phoned early Saturday, however, to change the hour to six.

I left somewhat early in order not to be late, and got to Grinzing, where Freud is staying, at five-thirty. I lingered in the car station awhile, then strolled up to the house. Anna Freud was just getting out of her car, and I accompanied her into the yard at the rear, where Frau Freud was sitting in a chair, quietly sewing. Dignified, shy, and gracious, she greeted me with a smile, and we exchanged a few words in English. She did not remember meeting me two years ago. She spoke of Berchtesgaden, where I had first seen the professor, and how beautiful it was there. "And now," she said, "Hitler lives there."

At six o'clock she went in, evidently to see if the professor was ready for me. A maid came a moment later and asked me into the house. Freud met me in the hall and shook my hand as we entered his office. He studied me for a moment and then said, "You look well." I sat on the couch, and we spoke for a few minutes, during which I told him I was staying for two weeks and that Margaret was here with me.

"Margaret is here with you," he repeated with interest. "I should like to see her."

83

I thanked him for this and then said, "I suppose I should lie down and just say what is in my mind."

"Yes," he replied, "do just what you would like to have your patients do."

I began by saying that since I had been there two years ago, I had experienced good fortune in my practice—due to the help I had received from him, to the assurance which those hours had given me, and perhaps also due to just good luck.

"You are now established in New York?"

"Yes," I said, "it seems so."

"Did you come for any special reason to see me?"

"No," I replied, "no special reason, except for the general help you can give and the joy that the hours bring to me."

I then spoke of Lourdes and our intention of going there when we left Vienna.

"Are you a Catholic?" he asked.

"No, I am nothing," I replied. "My religion is about like yours, as expressed in *The Future of an Illusion*. But I feel that average people cannot have such a bleak religion. Their minds are not well enough furnished. They must have an idealized father to depend on."

"You are probably right," he said.

Freud did not know of the medical board at Lourdes. When I spoke of the miracles, especially the cure of Pott's disease, he said, "I don't believe it."

I asked him what he thought of the so-called miracles. Were they mistakes on the part of the doctors? I said I felt sure they were not consciously dishonest.

Freud seemed doubtful as to this. It was not anything he said but an attitude that I could feel. Finally he said, "You know my prejudice. Probably functional conditions are helped, but I do not believe that Pott's disease can be cured."

I mentioned Carrel's assertion that he had seen varicose ulcers cured in twenty-four hours. Freud did not reply to this but made a gesture, as much as to say, "Don't know." When I added that Carrel believed people could be cured by prayer, the professor again made no reply.

I then spoke of hypnosis and the case of the man who was burned on the wrist, as given by Dr. Dunbar.

"These are authentic cases," said Freud. "I have seen such cases while I was with Bernheim."

During the hour, I spoke of Dr. Liddell's cases in his studies of animals: of the possibility of helping the pigs and sheep (who had nervous breakdowns) by a transference; and of the relation of psychoanalysis to this work. Freud seemed interested but did not reply.

I mentioned that Dr. Iago Galdston had been refused by the educational committee of the N. Y. Psychoanalytic Society, to which Freud said, "This seems a narrow viewpoint."

"I agree," I replied. Then I said that Iago had asked me if Freud would sign a book for him, that I had promised to transmit this request but that it would have to depend on whether Freud wished to do so. The professor did not reply to this . . . so that is off. (I had reminded him who Iago was and also about the Academy of Medicine in New York.)

I then spoke of the S. family, especially of T. Freud said, "Mrs. S. is a patient of mine."

"Yes," I replied, "Mr. S. told me, and she did also." I then continued, "My next thought is of Mr. S., who told me his mother had written you to ask if I was a good person for the treatment of stuttering and that you had said 'yes.' But when she asked if I was a good analyst, you had shaken your head. I replied that I knew how things are garbled in such a passage through two people, but that if it were so, I should not think any the less of the professor—only that he was wrong."

Freud replied that no such thing had happened. I then discussed some further technical aspects of the case, but Freud made only sparing comments.

Referring again to Lourdes, I said, "You must not think I am becoming 'religious.' Margaret is even more coldly scientific. She will be with me at Lourdes."

"Well," said Freud, "She will keep you from becoming too much so (religious)."

His final comment about Lourdes and the miracles was "As the Italians say, 'Perhaps no; perhaps yes.' "

We then discussed what hour would be most convenient. There was a choice of either 12 or 5, and I said I should prefer 12 o'clock. "Well, come Monday at 12," Freud said, "and I shall let you know. A gentleman has this hour, but I shall see if I can change it."

"Whatever is convenient for you," I replied, and with this I rose and shook his hand.

Freud appears to be even more energetic and alert than when I saw him two years ago. He seems very frail, but his movements are as quick as ever. And it was clear that his mind has lost none of its skill and cunning. His hearing seems slightly impaired but no worse than two years ago.

August 2, 1937

I had a restless night, due to some severe itching that has bothered me since I left New York two weeks ago but was able to keep the appointment.

The professor shook my hand as usual when I entered the room. I said as I sat down that Margaret was happy to accept his invitation and would come to see him at any time he wished. He said something about seeing her later.

There was some confusion when I asked whether my hour was fixed for 12 o'clock. Freud evidently thought I had reference to Margaret's appointment, which he said would be arranged for later. When I explained I was referring to my own hour, Freud said the other patient was ill, so that he had not yet had an opportunity to discuss the matter with him.

During the session, I brought up the question of why dreams were at times frank wish fulfillments. Freud spoke of children's dreams as being so. I said that I was referring to adult dreams and expressed the view that perhaps it is because in certain situations—as when men are starving or freezing or sick with loneliness—they must have this fantasy satisfaction in order to live.

Freud agreed but added that there is another element— that when the resistance is lowered, or when the wish is too strong for the censor, the wish comes out.

I suggested that perhaps this may be brought about by analysis—that is, we reduce the resistance by this means and so allow the wishes to come out in a frank form. "Yes," said Freud, "that is so."

As I left, he remarked, "I hope you will find this interesting."

The professor was wearing a dark checked suit or, rather, one with a small stripe in it, contrary to his usual pepper-and-salt suit. In fact, he was unusually well groomed today. Often he looks as though his suit needed pressing—although he is always immaculately clean.

August 3, 1937

Anna Freud phoned this morning and changed my hour to four instead of 12. It was a rainy day; when I reached the house, I stopped in the yard and waited under a dripping tree until my hour struck.

Before lying down on the couch, I asked Freud about a skin specialist. I told him I had seen Dr. Urback, who wanted me to go into the hospital but that I felt his pronouncement was too dogmatic. The professor gave me the name of Dr. Koenigstein. I then began my hour.

Margaret had said to me yesterday that because of the transference, it might be well for her to go to Paris for the two weeks I am here. She had suggested that I ask Freud about this and tell her just what he said. When I brought the question up today, Freud replied, "I could not say yes, and I could not say no."

"Margaret thinks the transference might interfere with the analysis," I said.

"I can see no relation to it," Freud replied. I told him I felt the same way.

I next spoke of seeing the parapsychology journal published at Duke University, and I mentioned Rhine's work there on clairvoyance and telepathy. The professor did not know of this work but was interested. Referring to telepathy and clairvoyance, he said, "There is something in it."

Next I mentioned the name of McCord of Albany, whereupon Freud said, "If you will open your eyes"—I keep a handkerchief over my eyes while associating—"you will see something he sent me."

I opened my eyes, and on a table in the middle of the

room I saw the bronze head of Freud that McCord had sculptured. (I had already seen another copy at the psychoanalytic association rooms in New York.) Freud evidently does not think it is a good likeness.

I said, "I think it is a poor likeness of you. There is something left out."

"Something put in, also," he remarked.

"I would recognize it, though, for you," I said.

"Would you recognize it for me?" he asked rather incredulously.

I had earlier compared the professor to Drummond, and I now remarked that in doing so I had made him (Freud) old and sick.

"You do not have to do this," Freud commented. "You find me this way."

"Oh, you are the same as when I saw you seven years ago," I replied.

"Was it so long ago?" he said. "When was it I first saw you?"

When I mentioned Berchtesgaden, he said, "Oh, yes, in the summer of 1929."

"You seem not a whit changed since then," I remarked.

"Only my hearing is not so good—or perhaps I should say, it is shorter," he replied. "It is useless to deny that I cannot understand you as well in English when you speak fast, or slur, especially when you use names."

"That is what you said about my speech seven years ago —that at times I spoke so fast and with such a slur that you could not understand me very well."

"Did I say that then?" he asked, somewhat eagerly and with pleasure in his voice. "Then perhaps it is not only hearing now." But he went on to say, "I must admit that my hearing grows poorer with the years."

At the end of the hour, the professor said, "Perhaps your dreams are preparing you for something."

August 4, 1937

When I went in today, I gave Freud the paper by Dr. Liddell on experimental neuroses in sheep. Freud glanced at it. "About sheep," he said and laid the paper on his table.

I then gave him a clipping about some work on psychic research done by a graduate student at Duke. Freud glanced at the title, "Spirit Research." "About spirits" was all he said.

Then he asked me if I had seen Koenigstein for my skin trouble yesterday.* I replied that I was to see him later in the day, and I thanked the professor again for giving me the name.

"Better wait and see what benefit you get" was Freud's response, so characteristic of him.

In the course of analyzing my dream I mentioned Monroe Meyer, whom the professor had analyzed. "Yes," Freud said, "he had a very satisfactory analysis."

"He is a very nice man," I remarked, "but in my opinion lacking in warmth." The professor said nothing.

I spoke of Lehrman. "He was with me for a season," said the professor.

I then went on to speak of Brill and added that Lehrman had told Brill I was only three weeks with Freud.

"He must have lied," said the professor.

*This proved to be an allergy to chocolate, of which I am very fond. I have been eating a lot of it this summer.

I then repeated one of the stories Meyer had told, supposedly about Freud—one of those apocryphal tales that are so often attached to great men. It was about an American patient who thought he spoke very fine German. During analysis, he heard the professor breathing regularly and deeply. The patient talked louder, but finally he heard the professor let out a little snore. Turning, the patient said, "Professor, you sleep."

"*Es macht nichts*" was the reply. ("It doesn't matter.")

When I had finished, Freud said, "It is not true. I never slept in my life in an analytical hour. . . . And if the man's German had not been good, I should have told him so."

Later, I spoke of working ten hours a day and this being too much.

"Well," said Freud, "I did it for many years . . . of course, not now."

August 5, 1937

When I came in today, Freud gave me back the clipping about psychic research. "You may ignore this about spirits, as it is not so," he remarked.

I then asked him if it were not worthwhile to study psychic phenomena in order to determine whether or not it was quackery, self-delusion, or some supernormal power.

"Yes, I suppose so," he said. "But it would take so much time to check up and to authenticate the facts that it would take a lifetime—and it would not be worth it. . . . Now, telepathy is a possibility and is worth study."

I then spoke of the need of studying the so-called miraculous cures at Lourdes, but he did not reply.

I talked about my patient, Mr. R.—of his brightness and also of his habit of arguing. The professor said, "Yes—some of these Eastern Jews are very bright." I went on to say how irritating this arguing was and asked Freud if he was ever irritated with patients. He laughed. "Sometimes," he said.

While I was waiting in the yard, before my hour, the professor came out on the porch and called to his dog, who was in the yard. When the dog came, he petted him on the head. It is not the same dog as two years ago—this one is a half-grown chow. The other dog, the professor told me, had died. I said, "It is hard to lose your dog."

"Yes," came the reply, "it is very hard."

Freud, I note, is still able to smoke and often does so during the hour.

August 6, 1937

One gets a feeling of increased power after these visits with the professor. They seem to cause a heightening of one's attention, and to bring to the surface relationships and new conceptions that had lain dormant before.

Today I was asked by the maid to come in by way of the porch, so that I had to enter the consultation room directly and put my hat and my book on the table in front of the professor.

"You are never without some printed material," Freud commented. (I don't know how he knew that I always have a book with me, since I leave it in the hall. The book is always the *Interpretation of Dreams*.)

"Yes," I replied, "this is my bible. I carry it and reread it every year." Freud looked at the book and grunted.

As I lay down, I said, "There is one passage in the book that I have just read, to the effect that when there is somatic anxiety, then infantile wishes that would cause a psychic anxiety use this somatic anxiety as a screen to come out. Is that right?" The reply was yes.

Then I asked about my patient, Mr. R., and his anxiety. I said, "In his case—as I see the situation—the primary state is an Oedipus, but he fears this and turns with special tender feelings to his father."

"Yes," Freud replied. "In general, the boy, because of his Oedipus relation to his mother, fears castration. But when he turns to his father, he also is castrated, since he must play the passive role. The boy either has an Oedipus relation to his mother, or he identifies himself with his mother."

A little later, he added, "When you find such anxiety as R. shows, you are always dealing with a castration fear."

August 7, 1937

Today I mentioned Dr. Liddell's paper on Pavlov, in which Liddell says that the main conditions for a neurosis in animals are restraint and confusion—except that I used the word "frustration."

Freud commented, "There is a German school that thinks of the neurosis as being caused by frustration." (He gave me the name.) "Further," he continued, "I think one could understand the neuroses of animals from studying the people with neuroses who have been analyzed."

August 9, 1937

Little to record about this session. I gave a dream but was unable to get anywhere with it. At the end, the professor said, "Tomorrow we must find the meaning of your fantasy." Half of the hour I spent telling him about Mr. S. Freud made practically no comment.*

August 10, 1937

Margaret made her visit today to see the professor, her appointment being at the beginning of my hour. She came out with me† and remained in the room with Freud for twenty minutes.

*I told Freud one day of Margaret's saying that if he had had the psychological need to form a philosophy of his teachings, what a following he would have, what a cult would have grown up about him!

†The dry weather had broken; it was raining but still hot. From the end of the car line there was a long climb up a tree-lined, curving road sunk below the level of the shaded yards which were held back by stone retaining walls. It was a bit like a paved moat. We were to wish many times later that it had been a moat with turrets and men strong enough to protect Freud and his work from being interfered with by violence. And yet we knew there was strength in the frail professor that was superior to violence and indifferent to it except as it might interfere with his work.

While Smiley stayed in the garden, I went in to say my farewells. The professor asked me to be seated near his desk. He looked at me a long minute. I thought, suddenly, that he did not recognize me, and I gave him my name.

"No, no," he said impatiently. "Of course I know you. I was just—just studying the change in you." Then he added, as if to right what might have seemed uncomplimentary, "But the eyes are the same."

He asked me about my work. "I understand that you are going on with the life of Thomas Becket." He asked me about my technique for research. I told him of the many contemporary lives of Becket and the wealth of material, and of the state of my manuscript. He listened with flattering intentness. I realized, with amusement, that again he was managing to make me feel as though he and I were

DIARY OF MY ANALYSIS WITH SIGMUND FREUD

When I went in, the professor was opening a reprint that had come to him in the mail. He came over, shook my hand, and said, "Well, Margaret is lively and full of life. I enjoyed seeing her."

"It will be a high point in her memory," I replied. "She appreciated the opportunity of seeing you."

"Well," said Freud, "when was it ever difficult for my friends to see me?"

---

equals, that of the two my work was even the more important. It is one of the moments of my life—a sort of accolade.

He told me of a novel in German about Becket—Konrad Meyer's *The Holy Man*. When I said that I was still clinging to source material as nearer the truth, he remarked that sometimes the poet (with whom he seemed to include the novelist) comes closer to the truth than the historian.

But the thesis of Meyer's novel, as Freud outlined it, was untenable to me, and I sidestepped an expression of opinion. He was searching in his bookcase in order to give me the exact reference. I could see only his back, and I was wishing that he would give up his quest for that reference and return to his chair. There were so many things that I wanted him to talk about! But I could hardly tell him that or imply that Becket, who had lived so famously in the eleventh century, was uninteresting as compared to him.

Finally, in order to get his mind off the novel, I remarked that in the source material two of Becket's dreams were extant.

"And," said Freud, turning quickly, "I suppose you will be able to interpret them?"

His sudden thrust put me on the defensive. I answered that I would hardly presume to undertake that since I was not even able to find out whether they were dreamed in French or Anglo-Saxon or Latin. I added, however, that I did know the size, shape, and name of the sword with which Becket, in his dream, had defended the king. (The sword was "Framea.") That did interest Freud, and he came away from the bookcase and sat down.

Smiley and I were about to leave for Lourdes—that astonishing shrine. Freud mentioned this and jokingly asked me if I would be able to preserve the family skepticism.

Then quite suddenly he rose, shook my hand, and in so doing led me to the door. He must have had a sense of the futility of lingering farewells. He had certainly developed a technique that would protect him from them, for no sooner was it time for you to go than you were out. And yet there was no feeling that you had been unwelcome but only that schedules were not made to be broken.—*M.G.B.*

August 11, 1937

When I went in today, I gave the professor the 1200 shillings for the 12 hours. "Is this the last day?" he asked.

"No," I said, "I come Friday—that makes twelve times. I just went to the bank today and got the money, so I felt it best to give it to you at this time." With a shrug, as though the money were of no importance, he laid it on the table.

"Well," he said, "we left some points to be discovered today."

"First," I began, "I want to ask you about the terminology 'dream content,' 'dream thoughts,' and 'dream material.' Are dream thoughts the associations to the manifest content?"

"The terminology is loose," said Freud, "but in general you can say that this is so."

"And is the dream material the meaning of the dream, apart from the stimulus of the dream?"

"It probably should include both the meaning of the dream (latent content) and the stimulus of the dream," he replied.

At another point in our discussion, Freud said, "When you find castration feelings in the man, in every case they go back to the primal scene, when the boy sees his father having relations with his mother and fears castration. Then there is an identification with the father in order to become more virile."

August 12, 1937

I asked the professor today about faith and suggestion but added, "Perhaps you may not want to answer this question."

"Why not?" he rejoined. "I shall if I can."

About faith, he said, "Of this I am sure: Faith represents a childish relation to the parent. To be sure, when it is to others, it may be, as you say, a transference of this parental faith to them. As for suggestion, we are not sure. It needs more elucidation. But of one thing I am sure—it is not an identification. Ferenczi said it was a childish relation; he reduced it to this. I do not disagree with him, but I am not sure."

I mentioned the arguments Margaret and I sometimes had on this subject. (I had taken the position that one could believe what one wished—as, for example, in God or in the Virgin Mary—as long as science did not disprove it.)

"I must take Margaret's side," said Freud. "You have no right to believe because of ignorance. Of course, if people believe this or that in their private lives, I would not fine or punish them. But scientifically they have no right."

August 13, 1937

This was my last session. I felt sad when I reached the house and sat waiting in the yard for my last meeting with the professor. It was quiet, the weather was cooler, and there was a peaceful air over the landscape. I heard a rooster crow several times, a dog barked some distance away, and there was the cry of strange large birds from distant trees.

After about ten minutes, the little maid I have known for so long ushered me into the house. I found the professor as usual in the room by his desk. I said good-day as usual, and he came over and shook my hand. As I sat on the couch, his dog came in, and I petted his head. "He knows me and has come to see me," I remarked. "Yes," said the professor, "he has come to see you."

I began by expressing the sadness I felt at having to go. Then I asked a couple of technical questions.

"Sometimes," I said, "I have patients who have such a resistance that they can't remember dreams, and as a temporary expedient I ask them to write down their dreams. Is this worthwhile?"

"No," replied Freud, "it is not worthwhile."

In answer to my second question, he said, "You cannot judge of a person's attitudes and needs through dreams alone. It is his whole life that you must take into consideration. A person may have a powerful trend and yet keep it in control; or a person may have a weak impulse and not keep it under control."

As I rose to go, Freud took my hand and came to the door with me. "Happy journey," he said in German, and then added, "Give my compliments to Margaret."

I said, "I should like to come back again."

"If I am here, you may," he replied. He then came out into the hall and turned to the porch, while I went out the other end of the hall.

As I went through the gate to the street and started down the hill, I looked at his study window. Freud was standing by the window, as on a former time, and waved me goodbye. I raised my hat, then went down the hill and to the car.

NOTE: 1938

The invasion of Austria by Hitler's troops in March, 1938, placed Freud in immediate danger. Previously, despite the anxious pleas of his friends, Freud had refused to consider leaving Vienna, where he had lived and worked for seventy-nine years. But now—when menacing visits from the Gestapo, detention of his daughter Anna for interrogation, and robbery of his household funds by gangs of Storm Troopers had transformed the Nazi threat into an ugly reality for his family as well as himself—he was finally prevailed upon to seek asylum in England.

It took months of delicate negotiations before this could be arranged. Ransom money had to be paid to the new barbarians, the psychoanalytic publishing firm's stock of books had to be delivered up for burning, and additional personal ignominies had to be endured without protest. Through the untiring efforts, however, of devoted colleagues and friends like Princess Marie Bonaparte of Greece, Dr. Ernest Jones, of London, and William C. Bullitt, our ambassador to France, the necessary exit permits were at last obtained. On June 4, with his wife and daughter, and accompanied by two faithful maidservants, Freud was finally allowed to cross the frontier into France and freedom. Two days later, after a stopover in Paris, Freud and his family arrived safely in London.

Like all his friends and admirers everywhere, we had been filled with deep concern about the professor's safety as we followed the grim events in the world press. When we finally learned that Freud had withstood the hardships of the journey and had even resumed analytic work in London, Smiley wrote to find out if he could visit the professor again during the summer. At first, because of Freud's uncertain health, there was some doubt as to whether this could be arranged. At the last moment, however, word came from the professor that he would have time for Smiley at the beginning of September, and in the latter part of August we sailed for England.

—M.G.B.

LONDON

August 30, 1938

We arrived in London Monday, August 29th, at five o'-clock. Went to the Whitehall Hotel, 4 Montague Street. I called Freud's residence at 39 Elsworthy Road but couldn't reach Anna Freud until the evening. She gave me an appointment with Freud for five o'clock the next day.

The house is on the edge of Primrose Hill. I arrived there a few minutes early and was admitted by Paula, the little German maid, who took my card to the professor. His office was just in front of the door, and I waited on the window seat.

The previous patient, a German-speaking man of middle age, left at five, and Freud came out into the hall to welcome me. He seemed as full of energy, as eager and as keen as I had ever seen him. His office opens on a garden

100

which runs down to Primrose Hill, with Regent's Park beyond.

Most of this first session was spent in talking about things that had happened since I had last seen him. I told the professor how distressed we had been over his plight and that once I even saw tears in Margaret's eyes when she thought of his condition in Vienna.

Freud made a sympathetic sound in his throat. "I was lucky that I was able to get out of Austria with comparative ease, due to the early and strong intervention from Washington," he said.

The professor confirmed that Ambassador Bullitt in France had telephoned Roosevelt and obtained the President's intervention on his behalf. "I got out, to be sure, with the loss of all my money," he said, "but yesterday all my furniture and collections arrived here in London."

In reply to my question, Freud also said it was true that Princess Marie Bonaparte had paid some of the ransom to get him out. Then he said, "We must talk of *your* person."

I told him of my work at the Marble Collegiate Church and also explained why I had written I would not come but then changed my mind when I got his letter.

The professor asked about Mr. S. and again wanted to know if he had any sign of dementia praecox (the mother insists that Mr. S. is crazy). I replied that there were no signs of any psychosis, and the professor said he was glad to hear it.

Freud then talked about the international situation, saying it was "quite serious."

"Yes," I said, "but I don't believe Hitler will go to war when he realizes he must face Russia, England, and France, with the sympathy and perhaps the economic and military help of the people of the United States."

"You cannot tell what a madman will do," replied Freud. "You know, he is an Austrian and lived for years in great misery in Austria. When he took over Austria, he seemed to be . . ." (I cannot recall Freud's exact phrase, but the idea was that it seemed "to go to his head.")

I suggested that Hitler's general staff, who are professional soldiers, and also his ministers would have a deterring effect upon him.

"Perhaps," Freud said. "But you can never tell what a man like that will do," he repeated.

"I understand," I remarked, "that Hitler has a personal dislike for you because of your teachings and because of psychoanalysis."

"I don't know," Freud rejoined, "but I hope so."

He then spoke of getting letters daily from Jewish friends in Austria, asking the Freuds to use their influence to help them. "You know," he said, "we are quite helpless to do anything for them."

In the middle of the hour, he interrupted me to say, "I have one more difficulty due to old age . . . excuse me." I correctly surmised that the difficulty was due to a slightly enlarged prostate.

The overall impression I get of Freud is one of keenness, cheerfulness, alertness, and even gaiety. Perhaps the universal regard which has been shown him in England, as well as the support of his friends during his difficult period in Austria, has stirred his spirit. When I said there was also widespread regard for him by people in the United States, he asked, "Do they seem more friendly to me and psychoanalysis?" I assured him of this.

When I referred to the incident of the Royal Society bringing him the book to sign because he was unable to go

102

out (a thing that had only happened before to royalty), he said, "Yes, I can show it to you." I suppose he meant the certificate they had given him.

"Are you allowed to work in England?" I asked.

"Yes," he replied with emphasis, "I can do everything." At the end of the hour, I brought up a dream which I hadn't had time to analyze very well. The professor said it seems to deal with repressions.

August 31, 1938

While waiting for the professor today, I chatted with Paula the maid. She spoke no English, so that I could understand only a little of what she said. While we were talking, Anna Freud came in. After the previous patient left, Paula preceded me into the room and made up the couch.

I spent the whole hour analyzing my dreams. They had to do with the desire to be closer to the professor, as well as an assumption in my unconscious of superiority over Freud and also a desire for youth. At the end of the hour, Freud observed, "You are like a boy again in your rejuvenation desires."

In the course of the hour, I asked him whether the regard and affection shown him in America made him feel differently toward us. (He has always expressed a certain antagonism against the United States and physicians in general.)

He answered, "No."

I noted the progress psychoanalysis was making in the U.S. and said, "I think that in the free spirit of a democracy like the United States, analysis could and is making good progress." There was no reply.

I then spoke of my work at the Marble Collegiate Church, of how I saw patients who were referred to me by the minister, and of my plan to write a book* with Dr. Peale —to write the psychiatric aspect of each subject (anxiety, alcoholism, etc.) and the minister to present his side.

"Do you think you can do it?" asked Freud. (He meant whether I could collaborate in a satisfactory way with a minister.)

I explained again that we would each take a topic and treat it according to our own viewpoint.

"Oh, yes," said Freud, "that seems quite possible."

I also said, "I see no reason why I should not do this church work without impairing my psychiatric standing and psychoanalytic standards." Freud replied, "I don't see why not."

In reply to another question by the professor, I explained that while I had an official position with the church, it did not pay anything.

"But it gives you reputation," he said in a tone of approbation. I said it did.

Then I spoke of our work at Lourdes and of the case of the Irishman who was healed and whom I had personally seen.

"Do you believe it?" asked Freud.

"Yes," I replied. "I cannot doubt the word of the physicians—reputable Irish doctors—who examined the case."

I got the impression that Freud was still skeptical, but he said nothing.

* *Faith Is the Answer.*

I then gave him our theory of the cure—that it was a transference to the ideal mother which originated the impulse to live. The professor said this seemed to be a reasonable thesis.

"This transference," I continued, "caused a marked hastening, I think, of the healing process." Then I said, "Primitive people often say they are going to die at some certain date and do die, and no cause can be found for their death." Freud said this is so.

"I don't know," I went on, "whether the immediate cause of death in their case is paralysis of the respiratory center or blocking of the heart muscle."

"At least," said Freud, "something happens, so they die."

In discussing some technical points later, I said, "When you are analyzing a person and you only have a few dreams, it is impossible to tell what the general trend of the patient's mind is. It only tells you what the patient is thinking at that time. You may not be able to tell how deep the feeling is, how continuous it is, and what influence it has on the patient's conscious mind."

"Yes, you are right," said the professor. "Dreams form a connected story."

"In other words," I said, "it is the general trend that is important and not some individual dreams?"

"Yes," said the professor.

My dreams for today were about the same as for yesterday. I analyzed part of the last dream but got bogged down toward the end of the hour. As I left, the professor said, "Perhaps the rest of the dream will be clear to you tomorrow."

September 1, 1938

At the start of today's session, the professor asked me if I had any more associations to yesterday's dream. "No," I said, "but I have three new dreams."

"Well, let's take them up," he said, and we spent the hour analyzing them.

The resistances were very great, and they continued until we could find the reasons for them. At the end, when I got the general meaning, Freud said, "You seem afraid of something."

At one point I kept trying to get at the meaning of a right-angled square, which had occurred in one of the dreams, until finally the professor said, "If you left it and came back to it, it would be easier."

It is Freud's custom never to let you keep plugging away at any item in a dream if you don't get it but rather to go on to the next point.

I noticed that Freud had a Pekinese dog, and I asked him about his chow.

"He—or rather, she—is in quarantine," he replied, "and will be out in three months. . . . This is a substitute dog." The Pekinese came up to my hand and licked my fingers. "She is very shy," said the professor.

During the hour, speaking of the time the Nazis marched into Austria on February 13,* I asked Freud whether he could continue to work.

"No," he replied, "I had two patients, but I dismissed them and told them to go away. When the conscious mind is troubled, one cannot be interested in the unconscious mind."

*Dr. Blanton was one month off. The Nazis entered Austria on March 12, 1938.—*Ed.*

"Could you continue to write?" I asked.

"Yes, I could write," he said. "There were some connections with the situation in Austria at that time and the material I was writing."

(Freud was working on the second part of *Moses and Monotheism*.)

September 2, 1938

Today I saw the professor in his temporary quarters at the Hotel Esplanade. He had told me the day before that he had to get out of his rented house but that the house he has bought, which is some distance away, was not yet ready for him to move in. The Esplanade is an émigré hotel kept by a Russian Jew.

I told the professor that Margaret was disturbed over the fact that he might have to eat English cooking. He replied that the hotel had a French chef and Margaret need not worry, as he would have excellent food. I said, "English food is awful." Freud agreed.

I said Margaret also is of the opinion that the English have rejected their nasal eroticism.

"Better say they have rejected their oral eroticism," said the professor.

"Yes, they may have," I agreed, "but as regards taste, the nasal part is the chief factor."

I spoke of my difficulties during the last session and recalled the professor's remark about my having something to conceal. "I have got something to say, and I may as well get it off my chest," I went on. "Perhaps this is what I am trying to conceal: It is my hope sometime in the future to retire to Nashville, Tennessee, where Vanderbilt University is. If I do, I might like to continue the work in analysis and perhaps found a psychoanalytic group there."

Freud asked at this point if Nashville was not a very small place. I explained that it is a town of 350,000 people, with three universities.

"Well," he said, "it seems it might be a good place, then, for that."

"Therefore," I continued, "I should like to become a training analyst, and perhaps you would not mind giving me a letter saying that you felt I was competent to do training analysis. This I can show to the committee of the New York Psychoanalytic Society."

"Perhaps you know that I have absolutely no influence with the American group," replied Freud. "There is a committee now appointed, of which my daughter is a member, to consider the relation of the American group to the international psychoanalytic group. The New York group is the strongest of the American groups and is more representative of them. They, the New York group, have just issued a statement in the nature of a declaration of independence —they cannot allow themselves to be controlled by the international group, and so forth. So, I could not give you a letter to be used with the New York society. They ignore my opinions. Brill apparently is the only friend I have in the New York group—or perhaps I should include Dr. Jelliffe. Probably the American group will secede; we expect it." He added that Dr. Brill had spoken of resigning from the New York group if they secede from the international group.

"If one wished, of course, to obtain a professorship of analysis in an American university," Freud continued, "I should be very glad to give it. But I can give you nothing to be used in connection with the New York group. I have no influence there." Freud seemed bitter about the matter as he spoke.

"Well," I said, "if you think I am competent as an analyst in general, and competent to be a training analyst in particular, I shall be satisfied."

"Yes," he said, "you are competent to do training analysis."

I then spoke of the desire I had to write an article about him, showing his character, his courage, his attitude.

"You are free to do as you like about it," he replied.

September 3, 1938

During today's session, I asked Freud if he would give me his opinion about a disagreement between Margaret and myself. In a recent story in the *Saturday Evening Post,* one of the characters, making fun of analysis, says, "You are a Freudian—you will not allow accident to account for a broken teacup or the slightest slip of the tongue!" I said that Margaret was more popish than the Pope. "She believes no accident can account for the broken teacup or the slip of the tongue."

Freud laughed. "Margaret is a clever girl," he said. Then he added, "As regards a teacup, I might allow accident for that—but not for the slip of the tongue."

"Do you think that an accident might account for a mistake on the typewriter?"

"That is not so clear," was Freud's reply—in other words,

it is not clear whether a typed error is always due to some unconscious motive.

During the session, I brought up the subject again of the New York group and remarked, "I feel they have a clique there."

"Do you feel yourself an outsider?" asked Freud.

"Yes, I do," I replied. "I feel that I don't belong."

The professor didn't say anything specific, but his exclamation and his manner indicated clearly that he felt I was justified in this feeling.

"As a whole," I continued, "I feel that they are a measly bunch. For example, Dr. Brunswick feels that L. is a good analyst, but I cannot think so."

"You cannot make me think so either," said Freud.

At the end of the hour, Freud said, "There is a difficulty about seeing you for the next few days. I must have another operation on my mouth. This will occur on Tuesday. I shall be away until Saturday. Perhaps I cannot work even on Saturday."

"Will you have a good surgeon?" I asked.

"We hope so. We have the first assistant of the surgeon I had in Vienna. The man is highly recommended to me."

"Are you in any discomfort now?" I inquired.

"No," he replied, "but there is a suspicious spot, and the surgeon thinks it should be removed. After such an operation I am in some discomfort, but not in any great pain." In a discouraged voice, he continued, "This is my twenty-second operation in fifteen years. It is a sarcoma, of course. It could not be very malignant, or it would not have lasted fifteen years."

The professor was 82 years old on May 6, 1938. The first operation therefore was at the age of sixty-seven.

September 5, 1938

The professor was his usual cheerful self. I first spoke of Bunyan's *Pilgrim's Progress,* a copy of which I had just bought. This year is the 250th anniversary of Bunyan's death. "Yes, I know the book," said Freud.

I spoke of Bunyan's genius, his lack of education, and how strange it was that he could write such a masterpiece.

"You do not need education to have genius," replied Freud.

I then cited Freud's statement in one of his books to the effect that the psychoanalyst cannot explain genius. Freud confirmed that this is so. I asked him if he remembered where he had written this.

"Probably in several places," he replied.

Discussing Bunyan's book, I referred to Mr. Fearing, who was so afraid of death, and I commented on how kindly Bunyan was in allowing the River of Death to be so low that Mr. Fearing went over hardly wet-shod. Here I mentioned the professor's own remarks on death.

"When you are my age," said Freud, "you think of death naturally. But those who think and speak of death are the ones who are not afraid of it. Those who will not speak or think of death are the ones who are afraid of it."

(In my previous notes, it will be recalled that the professor has often spoken of dying.)

I mentioned the professor's operation and the fact that he had aspiration pneumonia after such an operation once before, and I wondered if he would be in danger of it this time.

"No," said Freud, "I only had pneumonia once, and that was because the surgeon used too much adrenalin in the cocaine. This affected my heart, and afterward I had pneumonia."

Later, I remarked, "It seems to me that psychoanalysis tries to modify our hate and aggression, and religion tries to do the same thing." I added, "I don't know what you think of the comparison." The professor made no reply.

At another point, I said, "I feel that a lot of the benefit of psychoanalysis is due to the character of the analyst. . . . I think a great deal of the benefit I have had from my analysis is the association with you and the appreciation of your courage, your scientific manner, and your sympathy." Again Freud did not reply.

Speaking of our book on Lourdes, I said, "When our book is published, we shall be very much criticized by doctors."

"Yes, that is so," said Freud.

I spoke of Nunberg and of his being a good analyst. The professor agreed. I continued, "I think I shall consult him in connection with some problems about our book on Lourdes." Freud made an exclamation which meant that this would be wise.

In one of my earlier hours, I had spoken of my desire to play *The Merchant of Venice* in modern costume. I said that Shylock shows how Jews were persecuted, that when he wished to get the pound of flesh it was because he had been made mad by such persecution, and that Shakespeare had expressed his sympathy for the Jew in this play—as in the famous passage that begins, "Hath not a Jew eyes?" etc.

"Yes," said Freud, "Shylock has become modern again."

DIARY OF MY ANALYSIS WITH SIGMUND FREUD

September 6, 1938

Today Freud said his operation had been postponed for a day or so, and he would see me tomorrow. It seems the operation will be much more extensive than it had at first appeared, and he will be in the hospital for ten days. He asked me when I planned to return home, and I said on September 14.

"Ah," he said, "then tomorrow will probably be the last day."

"I feel justified in coming over for this short time," I said, "and I shall hope to come next year for even a longer time."

"I am afraid I shall not be here," replied Freud.

Later in the hour, I remarked, "You probably still feel some loyalty to Austria."

"Ah, no," he replied, "that is impossible. Austria is no more."

I asked him if he planned to become a British citizen.

"There is not time," he said. "It takes five years to become a citizen—but probably my family will become British citizens."

In the course of the session, I said, "Perhaps I am resentful in the unsconscious that you do not accept my case of the Irish boy who was healed. Perhaps I did not make it clear that he had records from three hospitals and that the doctors who gave him copies of the examination of his physical state did not know what might happen to him when he got to Lourdes."

"Well," said Freud, "I did not deny it." (He meant that he did not deny that the facts were as I presented them.)

The subject came up of the difference between Nazism and democracy. I said that in Nazism the citizen has no rights except those given him by the state, whereas in a democracy the citizen has certain inalienable rights given him by God Almighty—so that the Bible, in one sense, is the source of our democracy. The Bible teaches us that there is something due to Caesar and something due to God.

Freud made an exclamation of assent.

During the first part of the hour Freud had said that I might bring Margaret the next day. As I left, he repeated, "Now, don't forget to bring Margaret."

September 7, 1938

Margaret went with me today. Freud had visitors, and we had to wait in the corridor outside his door for several minutes until they left. Margaret then went in first and stayed for ten minutes.*

*Freud made me welcome and seated me by a desk covered with his books and personal effects and made bright with a bowl of white and red carnations. He was not distracted from his usual simple kindliness. He put me at ease at once and began asking me about the trip we had made meantime to Lourdes and added that he thought our thesis about the cures there tenable. He apologized for bringing Smiley all the way across the Atlantic and then having to cut short the work with him.

"Where will you go now?" he asked.

I told him that before going back to New York we would spend a few days in Stratford-on-Avon so that Smiley might poke around a bit and add to his Shakespearean lore.

"What!" he said with sudden and uncharacteristic sharpness. "Does Smiley really still believe those plays were written by that fellow at Stratford?" The professor knew and loved the plays as much as we could possibly have. It was "that fellow at Stratford" to whom he did not subscribe.

I should have loved to have told him about Smiley's "trial by fire" over his feeling about the Earl of Oxford. But I suddenly realized that if the professor had a sense of humor, I had never seen it manifest itself, and had I tried to tell him of Smiley's adolescent agony over that event, I think he would not have been amused.

When I came in, Freud seemed as full of energy and as cheerful as ever, in spite of the fact that he faced a severe operation the next day from which he might not recover. Two days before, when I had commented about his cheerfulness, Freud had replied, "Well, perhaps it is on the surface."

After I had settled down on the couch, Freud said, "This will be our last hour. My operation is in the morning, and I shall be in the hospital for a week or ten days. As you sail next Wednesday, we shall not be able to resume our hours."

I gave the professor the fee of 32 guineas for the time I had been there. It was in an envelope. Freud took the envelope in his hand and looked at it.

Freud then remarked that he was glad to see my own work going so easily. I had been working on a biography of Bernadette of Lourdes, and I asked him what he contemplated writing after his forthcoming book on Moses.

"Well, that's a trouble to me just now," he replied. "I have reached a place at which the writing does not seem to flow." It was an experience, we agreed, common to writers high or low. "But" he added, "nonetheless painful."

We talked a while about Smiley, he asking me questions about Smiley's personal life and especially about his opinions—about Lourdes and the cures. I then told Freud how we had worried about him all spring until we heard that he was in England.

"Yes, that is the pleasant aspect—England. But only to have this operation! That is not so happy." He moved his expressive hands. His face was troubled. "It is the over-and-over part of it that is so bad. The again and again." And he added something which I did not quite get, to the effect that perhaps I had come to see him for the last time.

I got up to leave. We shook hands, and remembering the smooth swiftness with which he terminated interviews, I started for the door.

But a slight sound checked me, and I turned. He was standing by the bowl of carnations, carefully selecting for me two, one of each color, perfect and in full bloom.

It was almost intolerable to leave him there—an aged and ill exile among unhappy fellow exiles.

But somehow Freud could never really be aged and ill. In his small body but great presence he was always to us the great explorer into the dark continent of the unconscious mind.

Eventually posterity may even remember his generation because it was his, and twentieth-century Vienna because it was dominated by him, just as one says, "Assisi of St. Francis," in saying, "St. Francis of Assisi."—*M.G.B.*

"This," he said, "will pay for a week in the hospital."

"I hope you will not think I am presumptuous," I said, "but if you need some money, since you have been robbed of all your money in Austria, I can arrange to let you have it."

"Ah, no," he said pleasantly.

I began my hour by saying that I had three dreams at different sleeping periods during the night.

"I presume even if dreams occur at different sleep periods during the same night," I said, "that they are all connected, just as if they had all occurred during the same sleep period."

Freud said my presumption was correct.

"In the last dream," I continued, "I seem to be successful, and have a feeling of good luck. . . . I venture to prophesy that your operation will go all right."

"Well, perhaps it's a wish fulfillment on your part," said Freud.

"Perhaps it is only superstition," I replied, "but I still feel your operation will turn out all right."

One of my dreams had to do with the fear of homosexual attack on me.

"That," said Freud, "is the cause of the greatest resistance and fear in men."

I asked the professor why he felt that lay analysts were essential for the advance of psychoanalysis.

"Because," said Freud, "the psychiatrist who takes up psychoanalysis is interested in the therapeutic needs chiefly. This aim is not to be disparaged, but it is not the main or even the essential aim of psychoanalysis. The chief aim of psychoanalysis is to contribute to the science of psychology and to the world of literature and life in general."

"In other words," I said, "the psychiatrist who engrafts

116

psychoanalysis onto his method is interested chiefly in therapy, while the lay analyst may be more interested in research."

"Yes," he said, "that's true."

Referring to the New York laws against lay analysts, I said, "I am sure you must appreciate that even if the New York group wished to have lay analysts, it would be difficult under the law."

"It is due to the attitude of the New York psychoanalytic group that such laws have been passed," Freud replied.

I agreed this might be so.

"In England," Freud continued, "there is complete freedom to do lay analysis. All they have to do is to say they will not sign a prescription or prescribe for their patients, and they can practice freely."

I asked Freud if the British group of analysts felt they were dominated by the International Psychoanalytic Association.

"No," he replied.

"Then it seems to be the custom of Jewish people to destroy, to cast out, to kill their teachers," I said. "They stoned the prophets and crucified their great teacher."

"The American group is largely Jewish, dominated by Rado," said Freud, "while the Americans"—meaning the Gentiles—"do not seem much better."

"Well, perhaps not just now," I replied. "But later they may turn out better and advance the science of psychoanalysis."

"Let us hope so," said Freud.

When I got up to leave, he added, "Well, maybe you are the one who may advance the science of psychoanalysis."

I then spoke of the good I had got from him—not simply from what he had said but from his character and attitude.

I spoke of the need of men between 55 and 60 to get a philosophy that will enable them to go on confidently and contentedly. Quoting the lines from "Rabbi Ben Ezra" ("Grow old along with me! The best is yet to be"), I said, "I don't think this is so. I don't think the best will come at fifty or sixty. If you are any good, you are at the best of life when you are around thirty to forty."

"You are right," said Freud.

"But at least," I went on, "we can go along contentedly if we we get the right philosophy. As Shakespeare said, 'Cowards die many times before their deaths,' and when one reaches the age of death, it is easy to die." And again I quoted Shakespeare: "Men must endure their going hence, even as their coming hither: Ripeness is all."

I then spoke of Margaret, saying that if her book were successful, she would be less timid about her work.

"Don't you think it will be successful?" Freud asked, his tone of voice indicating that he did not doubt it.

"Yes," I replied, "I think it will be."

"I think she will be successful," said Freud—meaning in her work and with this book in particular. "You can tell her so, if you wish."

As I finally moved to go, Freud slapped his hand into mine and said, "I should be glad to see you, if I am able, any time you come. . . . Good-bye!"

How different this scene of parting, at the Esplanade Hotel, from the two partings before in the old wine village of Grinzing! Since I had seen Freud the year before, the whole world had turned over.

BIOGRAPHICAL NOTES AND COMMENTS

by Margaret Gray Blanton

In working over and footnoting this material, I have become increasingly conscious of the fact that from this diary one would get a very one-sided and perhaps distorted picture of my husband.

So, perhaps a few words are needed about his origins and early training.

Smiley had always insisted that eventually he would write an autobiography, with special emphasis on the education of a person completely immersed in the Civil War history and the frontier history of the mid-South state of Tennessee. He had even discussed it with publishers.

His people had come to the Nashville area from Virginia and Maryland, and knew the history and tradition of the Revolutionary War and the War of 1812 in which many of them had been soldiers. His ethnic inheritance was English, Scotch, Irish, Welsh, and Border with a strong addition of Huguenot French.

And in the South, of such a group one very rightly says "the family," for the family was a very basic unit, built on the plan of the clan and carrying both its faults and its virtues. It is certain that once a member always a member, for next to country the family held a man's strongest loyalty.

The whole Nashville area, in which he was reared, had

been occupied by troops during the Civil War, and it would have been hard to rest along a fence row without picking up a souvenir of the fighting. Children hunted for bullets instead of four-leaf clovers.

Smiley's great grandfather, Meredith Blanton, came from Cumberland County, Virginia, immediately after the War of 1812 in which he had served. Meredith settled in the place near Shelbyville which came to be known as Unionville. In May, of 1882, Smiley was born there. His mother, Sarah Araminta Brunson—Sally as she was called—of Huguenot stock had come there to teach. When Smiley was still an infant, they moved to the home of a widowed sister of his mother's in Pennington's Bend of the Cumberland River.

There Smiley's mother died, and his father married the widow Pennington, who was Sally Brunson's sister. From the Bend, after so long, the family moved to the old Foster house, on Murfreesboro Pike, built in 1828, in the environs of Nashville, near where the rest of the family had originally settled.

Smiley was the only child among five adults of his own family and two adult Negroes who had been with the family since slavery days.

His most important playmates, through all his earliest years, were the various animals on the place but most of all an imaginary dog called Nooks. Nooks slept with him, sat with him, romped with him, and was fed at the table. The imaginary dog became so real to the family that some of them remembered it as a real animal. It eventually died, and a funeral was held for it, in the rose garden, attended by the family.

The whole group adored Smiley, and Smiley always felt that he had been badly spoiled. People who observed the situation did not think so. They thought that he had been overcontrolled, overmanaged, and overloved, and that the family had developed in him a tenacity and stubbornness for which he paid with much of his energy and often with his health. While he was young, he had tuberculosis, of which his mother had died, and he survived malaria, which was endemic in that section of the South.

Children in Nashville did not go to school very early. Smiley started at the usual seventh year. He had already learned to read, and he became an extremely rapid and even an obsessive reader. There was an unused attic room in the huge old house where they lived, and when he was pressed by the surrounding wall of adults, this was his refuge. The attic was full of discarded books, including much poetry and many magazines. There were featherbeds to burrow into and low windows looking out onto the Cumberland foothills which became Smiley's ideal of "mountains."

This was Smiley's weekend retreat. And the rule of this Presbyterian household—only the Bible or Shakespeare on Sunday—gave him a delightful excuse for retreat.

At eight Smiley joined the church, "by default" as he put it. On Sundays he went to a small nearby Methodist church, on Murfreesboro Pike, called Arlington. One Sunday during a "protracted meeting" his exceptionally pretty sixteen-year-old Sunday school teacher kissed him and asked him if he did not want to go to Heaven. Smiley, who could never have resisted this under any circumstances, promptly joined. But one of the most painful moments of his childhood was the complete silence that followed his announcement at the dinner table on his return home. Only the youngish "war" uncle looked amused instead of shocked. The conflict of this situation left him without affiliation, and he was almost sixty before he became connected with a church, and then it was of the Protestant Episcopal denomination.

In school he was never especially liked. He was obsessed with the necessity for "doing it his own way," and he asked questions and held opinions that were the despair of his instructors. However, in English and in history he excelled.

His great hero, as he was growing up, was Andrew Jackson, the popular idol. Very early he showed a tenacity of memory. Once learned, a fact was always there, however unimportant. He could recall such minutiae as the number of cannons employed in a given battle.

"THE War," as it was called in the South, ended only seventeen years before Smiley's birth, but not a great length of time to the long-memoried South. To him the battles and the campaigns seemed like an enormous war game.

He told of seeing the Confederate monument dedicated in Mount Olivet Cemetery (very close to where he now lies) and of seeing the large crowd weeping for the "Lost Cause." He was puzzled that he felt no great grief—only sympathy for the people who remembered so well. And he remembered that on the way home, he had thought, as he pedaled his way through the haunted, leafy lanes, that the war's loss had been for the best. And he had also realized that he must not say so out loud.

When he had finished grade school, he was told firmly by all concerned that he must not try the equivalent of high school, that his health was too precarious. He said that he did not put up any argument whatsoever, but on the day of registration at Montgomery Bell Academy he rode the four miles on his wheel and registered.

His four years there were not very successful either. He said he barely "squeaked through," and when he asked for a copy of his grades to present to Vanderbilt University for entrance, he had the chagrin of being told by the head that he should not try it. When he persisted and asked why, he was told quite bluntly that he was "too big a fool" to make it.

He took the papers to Vanderbilt, however, and there he had a great piece of luck, almost his first, academically—he came under the guidance of Dr. Richard Jones.

In 1904, he graduated and took his B.S., again by a somewhat narrow squeak. This time it was due to his inability to learn German and his great dislike of it. He had a slight knowledge of French, however, and he liked the sciences. From there he went to Boston where he studied graduate English at Harvard and registered in Dr. Curry's dramatic school.

In this period, he became interested in speech defects, especially stuttering. He was too perceptive to accept stuttering as a defect of speech in itself and found himself aiming at a medical degree and psychiatry. He often said that however long it took him to get pointed in the right direction, there had never been a turning in his whole life that had not moved him toward it.

He was, however, without funds. So he planned to teach in order to save. He applied first to the Culver Military Academy for a position in public speaking. But much to his amusement in later years, his application was turned down because he misspelled "professor" with two *f*'s. Then he applied to Cornell at Ithaca, where he was accepted.

In addition to teaching as an instructor, he took his first year of medical work and a year in neurology, and he organized the Cornell Dramatic Club.

In 1909 Smiley and I met. My home was in Nashville

where his people still lived. We drove by the hour through all the leafy lanes around Nashville and explored in detail the field of the battle of Nashville. I could not say that I was not forewarned.

My father died in the fall of 1910, and Smiley and I, on his salary of eight hundred dollars a year, were married and began to plan for the rest of his three years of medicine.

Academic life at Ithaca offered much satisfaction, but Smiley had decided to study medicine and then get training in psychiatry, so in 1911 we moved to New York City, where he entered Cornell Medical School. He was twenty-nine, and we had the sum of $115 a month to see us through the three remaining years. Dean Kerr got him a scholarship.

We were very happy and often very hungry, but we never regretted it. And a top-floor rear of an unheated rooming house on East 32nd Street did not frighten me then as it would now.

I very quickly realized that if I were going to survive with Smiley, I must learn what I could of the things he was at work on. I was right in that, and I persisted in it to the time of his death.

In addition, I learned to write, and during that period published some fourteen articles. Writing was not a very well-paid profession then. For the top article I received twenty dollars.

When he graduated in 1914, we went to the University of Wisconsin where he established a speech and mental hygiene clinic in the Department of Public Speaking.

We then took into our family Smiley's devoted step-mother, who was completely paralyzed. We were at Wisconsin nominally ten years, from 1914 to 1924. But during that time we went on leave to Phipps Psychiatric Clinic,

Johns Hopkins Hospital, Baltimore, to study. Smiley was with Dr. Adolph Meyer, and I researched under Dr. John Watson for whom I did a study, "The Behavior of the Human Infant During the First 30 Days of Life."

In 1917 Smiley went into the army in a special medical section of psychiatrists. In 1918, as Captain Blanton, he went to France at the head of a group of psychiatrists and assistants and nurses. He was assigned to the 2nd Division, and when the war ended, he was in a forward trench just behind the front lines. He was in some of the heaviest fighting.

He was then sent into Germany, to Trier, to study the mental status of small schoolchildren.

After his return we were briefly at Wisconsin again, but Smiley decided to go to London to take the Royal College examinations in neurology and psychiatry. He worked at Madeline Hospital and at Queens Square.

While we were there, I went to the University of London where I worked in phonetics under Dr. Daniel Jones.

Again back to Wisconsin and from there in 1924 to Minneapolis, where he started the child guidance clinic in the public schools.

There we wrote a book together for teachers and parents, called *Child Guidance*. In 1927 we went to Vassar College at Poughkeepsie, where Smiley headed the nursery school that they were opening.

That unfortunately did not work out, and it was from there in the fall of 1929, only a few weeks before the break in the market that we went to Vienna to work with Professor Freud.

We did not realize, no one did realize, that the Depression had started. For a while one only knew that things had happened to "the market," and as far as the market was concerned, it had never been an entire reality for average people.

Fortunately for us, our resources had been put into letters of credit from top banks, and at that period the banks had not yet begun going under. So we lived comfortably and were able to pack our anxieties into our analytical hours, which, since we could not do anything about the approaching Depression, was all to the good.

Smiley's friends have asked me to discuss several phases of Smiley's life that I do not feel entirely competent to discuss. Nevertheless, I shall do what I can. One field was Smiley's religious attitude, another was the observable reaction to his analysis, and a third was a fantasy life that he added to his normal one. These are all very subjective fields, and of course I must be limited to what I recall his having said or done in connection with them.

Smiley and I sat and talked rather more than most married couples did, I suspect. Smiley often commented on it with amusement.

We had certain "rules" of procedure, however. We might discuss debatable things in the morning when we first got up, might even quarrel a bit, although we always parted with a caress. But when Smiley came home from the office at night, we rigidly adhered to the best and politest "company" manners that we could muster, and we tried to make the dinner hour as interesting and relaxing as possible. The only exception to this was a deliberate show of temper on my part if he were late. Four minutes I could tolerate. Seven minutes, maybe. But ten minutes and a tantrum! And I used my best dramatic capacity on those tantrums.

Whatever Smiley was with other people, he was always late with me. Through most of our life together, I did the dinner cooking. I got so I did it pretty well, and to have it delayed ruined it and angered me. Also, he tended to work too late for his own good.

When he was late, he tried various diverting tactics such as the old one of throwing in his hat. And if he were late enough, I put on a show for him and threw it back out.

Smiley's temper was evener than mine. He was polite enough to say that it was just that my reaction time was somewhat too short. But, he added, since I did not pout, a short reaction time merely added to the excitement of our relationship. Pouting on the part of either of us was to be considered cause for divorce.

When he came in within time limits, he usually swaggered in, referring to himself as Smiley Always-on-Time Blanton or variations, and we made light of it. During dinner we discussed the interesting things that had happened during the day, sometimes scraping the bottom of the barrel.

Even during the wars we brought very little of that to the table. And news broadcasts were tabu. We never discussed finances, however low they might be, at the time.

Of course such rigid rules often left us falling back on abstractions, and since Smiley read at any available moment, night or day, and read extremely widely, that was not too difficult.

What I heard of his religious convictions usually came up at this time. After dinner, the talk often continued into much of the night, and it covered a large field.

The thing that I recall most vividly was his continued wonder that Christianity had survived in the face of the continual violations of what Christ taught. That, he considered, was the one basic reason for the existence of the church, and he came back, over and over, to what he considered the dominating philosophy: "Love thy neighbour as thyself." So far as he was concerned, he said, this covered it all. To him the ideas evolved by the church doctors meant nothing. He did not care for and never could be persuaded to accept any rigid man-made creed which he referred to as "the quibbles." It was in this context that he would say, to the distress of his friends, that he had no religion.

He admired Saint Paul very much, primarily because of his beautiful writing. I did not, because of his attitude toward women, and it was a common cause of disagreement between us.

Perhaps it was not as simple as that may sound, for Smiley and I had one subject on which we not only could never agree, which we even had to rule out for discussion: the place of women in Western society. From my earliest memory, I had been an ardent feminist. Smiley, I felt, flatly disagreed with that cause.

When I would get onto that subject, Smiley would exclaim, "There you go on your obsession!" And I would answer, "Go ahead and say the rest of that speech," and he would! "Well, you know as well as I do that woman is man's superior," which always made me want to hit out—or to at least slam doors. If he had said "man's equal," I would have thanked him for the compliment. But he never did. He just would say "superior," which I knew he did not really think.

I spent hours trying to convince him that one of the basic troubles with society today is man's inability to believe in the equality of the sexes and his need to downgrade the sex of his mother. I never succeeded, but I never gave up trying. Then he would enrage me, giving me whimsical answers!

He was fond of whimsy. Especially about animals. The Uncle Remus influence, he said. All animals were people to him, and whenever "conversation would run low in the bin," as he was fond of quoting from Uncle Remus, he would fall back on a whole world of "play pals." Mrs. Mouse he delighted in, as, incidentally, he did in real mice. But he depended on me to weave a plot around them. He used to say that it was inevitable that he should have married a fiction writer. If I had not been one, I should have had to become one.

He discussed this with Professor Freud, once, whose comment was "You obviously married Scheherazade."

When he lay dying, he took a notion to do without a night nurse. He tried to outargue me about it. Finally I fell back on Mrs. Mouse. If he had no night nurse, how could Mrs. Mouse get in to see him? And she was already having trouble, as there was no safe place for her to stay in his room since she usually lived in his bedroom slipper. He was quiet for a while. Then he put his hand under his pillow where he kept a very small flashlight. "She can come here and stay right with the flashlight," he said. "I'll have her to talk to in the night."

If these seem to be rather superficial things to write down about him, they are not. He reminded me one day that a man who listens to other people's troubles all the time needs a world of fantasy to escape into. And that he had.

Of any writing that I have done here, this chapter will be the most inadequate because the least objective. But everyone who has handled the manuscript thinks it necessary for some evaluation to be made of the effect of his analysis on him.

It will also be the most difficult, partly because I had been in analysis myself at the same time, and it is hard to untangle the changes in two people and assess them. It takes me also into a discussion of our relationship before analysis as compared with afterward, and of certain things that I saw as temperamental changes due to it.

He had many contradictions in his makeup. For instance, he knew exactly what he wanted to do and how he meant to go about doing it, no timidity whatsoever. But because certain parts of his education had been neglected—music for instance and the arts and architecture—and because they happened to have been my strong points educationally, he would make himself entirely dependent on my opinions. I had actually to be on guard about expressing a casual opinion, or presently I would hear him quoting me as expressing a certainty.

His mind was intent on the new depth studies in behavior and was channelized, whereas my education in this line had been much neglected. I would take up some study for a couple of intensive years and then have ideas and opinions and scatter them regardless.

I once, for instance, spent some time on a study of the rivers of the country. Smiley loved to hear me talk about them, although his real love was the mountains. Or again when we were in England, I spent an intensive period studying the architecture of the Cotswold country, while he walked the Wye Valley and learned its history. We would share our findings and learn from each other.

We both loved the history of the South, but we differed even there. My interest was mainly in the settlement and what one might call folk history. He knew "the War" by heart.

Our close interests, which were still diversified, made for much exciting talk. We were both "brain pickers."

Smiley was always unexpected and arresting. And he was never a bore. You might like him or dislike him, but no one was indifferent to him. I never once saw him come where I was, without pleasure, or saw him leave without regret. Conversation between us was always valuable and always easy. We speculated on things and causes and behavior—and formed theories. That was in the first part of our marriage!

And then after twenty years of marriage we were both analyzed—and another Smiley developed and doubtless another me.

Two things had happened to him. First, there were changes in his appreciation of his own family. For instance he had always been very devoted to his grandmother, Emily Brunson, and awed by her. She was a very formidable little person, a very loving person to him but also very aggressive. It always seemed to me that she had two destructive traits. She always knew best, and she nagged Smiley to live up to her ideals.

His father was a somewhat shadowy figure to him. They loved each other dearly, and his father did everything he could do for his son, but they had practically nothing in common except their past. Their conversation always fell back on reminiscence.

And then he was analyzed, and Professor Freud became his beloved father figure, and his grandmother and I, who had been identified with his grandmother, were dethroned. His necessity to accept everything that I said as gospel truth was dispelled, and he became very negative. Of course it is probable that changes in me that I cannot see were factors also. But I do know that thereafter my role became entirely different.

We had to quit writing books and articles together, and I had to guard my every statement.

During the first of this period, we fell back on reading.

But this worked poorly, because Smiley felt guilty at our lack of verbal contact, and took to reading out loud to me.

This reading aloud was the closest we ever came to breaking up our marriage. That was partly due to a misjudgment on my part. I conceived the idea that if I gave him the complete set of Freeman's *Lee,* he would be so eager to read it that he would read to himself for speed.

But I was mistaken in that. And I reached the end of my endurance one night when a dinner cook left shaking with laughter because every night, she said, she left me "burying the Confederate dead."

I took a twenty-eight-day boat to Plymouth, England, and agreed to consider coming back when he had finished. I stayed several months in London where I worked at the British Museum library. I was looking up data for a possible life of Thomas Becket and Henry II.

He wrote me his usual charming letters and forswore ever reading aloud to me again. He went overboard! He found us a new apartment, bought a new car and a new pet, an African gray parrot. And I returned.

But unfortunately Freeman had also written a *Washington!* So I had to try another tack to coax him away from reading aloud. I finally invented a whole world of imaginary playmates for him, and when he came in for dinner, or in the night when we would both be wakeful, our lives would be filled with the exploits of Mrs. Mouse who had just decided to compete with the Duchess of Windsor or who had tried to lick a police officer whom we both knew at a local corner. This continued for the rest of our lives.

Of course we still had a great deal in common. For instance we both had a passionate love of good food, in a town full of good restaurants large and small.

At that time Smiley became an almost obsessive golfer,

and I have no capacity for sports. But we would go away on golfing trips together, I with a suitcase of historical records to arrange and record, he with a huge bag full of clubs.

He loved his Sleepy Hollow Club, shuttled back and forth between it and Thunderbird Club in Palm Springs, California.

His greatest interest of course was the American Foundation of Religion and Psychiatry that he and Dr. Peale were organizing. He thought it antisocial that these two integral parts of our culture were not coordinated.

After I quit writing with him, he and Dr. Peale wrote two books together.

Then he began to write on his own, and I began to write alone also. His best book I think was *Love or Perish.* My one biography was of Bernadette, the "poor little saint" of Lourdes. And a novel called *The White Unicorn,* a picture of the South in the 1890's.

Smiley did a collection of familiar poems for people in trouble to read. Poetry was so much a part of his life that he could not imagine a life without it. He remembered an enormous lot of it and most of it with great accuracy.

Smiley and I had several customs that were almost rituals. He never left the house without our exchanging a tender good-bye. And he had an unbreakable rule that one must never take his wrath to bed with him. No matter what had occurred between us, he came to me before we went to sleep and said an "I'm sorry; let's forget it." He was often more generous than I was!

He was not too good a sleeper, and he would wake in the night and read. When the light had been coming from under his door for what seemed to me a long enough time, I would go in and sit on the side of his bed and try to coax him to sleep by diversions. I always found him propped up on a stack of pillows, a strong light bent over his book and a soft felt hat drawn over his eyes to shade them.

One night at the end of October, it was about three when I went in. I asked him if he had been reading a certain book on sleep.

"Finished it," he said, "and I got up and got this." It was one of the oldest lives of Lee that he had. "Now," he challenged me, "you are critical of the way he conducted the battle of Sharpsburg."

"Yes," I answered, springing to my own defense and taking up the argument where we had last laid it down. "Lee fought that battle with his back to the river, and no bridges and no boats."

"Oh, yes!" Smiley came back, "but he was fortified with a thorough knowledge of his opponent! He had gone to West Point with him. He knew that when that man got his men up to the ground near the field, he would have them all rest. And that his own men [Lee's] could be readied to fight come daybreak. You ought to be well enough informed by now to know they couldn't have caught the old fox! It just couldn't be done!"

I took the book away from him, and he let me, and I removed his felt eye shade and straightened his cover.

"Mark the place!" he said. "They couldn't get the best of the Old Man!"

The next day we had luncheon at the Metropolitan Club and strangely enough talked mostly about the possibility of life after death. Then we walked toward home in the sun, and he commented on how wonderful it was to walk in the autumn sunlight together. At the corner we touched hands as we always did in parting.

Thirty-six hours later he was gone.

I had for many years been Smiley's shadow. For years,

indeed I had been known as Smiley's Margaret. I even signed myself so at times. Now indeed I was to take up that role in earnest.

He is buried with his family, under the trees that he loved and in sight of the foothills that shaped his childhood.

—M.G.B.

INDEX